"Any reader of this volume will find themselves more comfortable with data and perceived by others as more competent in making data-driven decisions. It is a small investment with a high payoff for individuals, their present or future organizations, and the citizens they serve…It is a necessary complement to courses on statistics or quantitative decision making, and should become widely adopted in Public Administration, Public Policy and Nonprofit programs, as well as many professional degrees."

From the Foreword by Marc Holzer, Founding Dean and Professor Emeritus, School of Public Affairs and Administration, Rutgers University, USA; Founder, National Center for Public Performance

"I have seen the effects of data fear many times throughout my career in public service. Anne and Ron offer practical approaches to alleviating these fears both at the individual and organizational level. This book is a critical read for anyone who wants to overcome data fear in themselves or others."

Toni Harp, former Mayor of New Haven (2014–2020), USA; Connecticut State Senator (retired); Chair, Appropriations Committee

"Working with both Anne and Ron on many initiatives, I have gained a real appreciation for how powerful data can be in convincing key decision makers to embrace change. New public policies and investments must be rooted in data and then continually measured to ensure effectiveness and public support. The book is a must read."

William Carbone, Distinguished Lecturer, Executive Director of Justice Programs and The Tow Youth Justice Institute, University of New Haven, USA; Executive Director (retired), Court Support Services Division, Connecticut Judicial Branch

Working with Data in the Public Sector

Working with Data in the Public Sector: From Fear to Enthusiasm is the first book designed for practicing and future public administration professionals to help overcome any anxiety about using data effectively in their roles.

Authors Anne McIntyre-Lahner and Ronald Schack explore different types and degrees of data fear (a data fear/data comfort continuum) and provide a toolbox of fear-fighting techniques, including methods of dealing with data fear "in the moment," methods of mitigating data fear related to using, sharing, and reporting data, and demonstrating how many common data tasks need not be scary. They further offer a self-assessment instrument and process to help individuals assess their level of data fear/comfort, identifying which specific dimensions of data fear/comfort may be most problematic at both the individual and organizational levels. The book examines how individual data fear can "infect" organizations, collaboratives, and communities and how to "bake in" data fear prevention in one's efforts to create and sustain a data-informed culture.

It is important reading for both practicing and future public servants, including those enrolled in public administration, public policy, and nonprofit management programs.

Anne McIntyre-Lahner is CEO of Action 2 Outcomes and Adjunct Professor in the School of Public Policy at the University of Connecticut, USA.

Ronald W. Schack is Managing Director of The Charter Oak Group, LLC, and Adjunct Professor in the School of Public Policy at the University of Connecticut, USA. He holds a doctoral degree in Political Science from the University of Connecticut.

Working with Data in the Public Sector

From Fear to Enthusiasm

Anne McIntyre-Lahner and Ronald W. Schack

Routledge
Taylor & Francis Group

NEW YORK AND LONDON

Designed cover image: © Getty Images

First published 2025
by Routledge
605 Third Avenue, New York, NY 10158

and by Routledge
4 Park Square, Milton Park, Abingdon, Oxon, OX14 4RN

Routledge is an imprint of the Taylor & Francis Group, an informa business

ISBN: 978-1-032-80304-3 (hbk)
ISBN: 978-1-032-80302-9 (pbk)
ISBN: 978-1-003-49632-8 (ebk)

DOI: 10.4324/9781003496328

Typeset in Palatino LT Std
by codeMantra

Contents

Foreword

Although we live in a data-driven world, fear of data erodes the power of that body of evidence. Decision-makers are often reluctant to share performance data with their stakeholders for fear of being criticized: "We had no control over the outcomes." "The public (and their media surrogates) wouldn't understand the numbers." "The data does not represent our current progress."

Such fears are common. At the same time, they constrain opportunities for improvement. Analogous to the medical model, ignorance of an organization's improving or declining health only leads to missed opportunities to deliver goods and services as promised. Remediation becomes more expensive. Progress becomes more difficult. Mediocrity becomes more likely.

Fortunately, Anne McIntyre-Lehner and Ronald Schack have confronted these problems – often characterized as the "digital divide" – head-on. In a text with wide appeal to professionals, data analysts, and colleagues who are data-averse, they draw a clear schematic for instilling a data-driven culture in the workforce.

The ability to wield data as a diagnostic problem-solving competency is at the core of this short volume. It is a competency that many professionals lack, one that must become more apparent in graduate and undergraduate courses across a wide range of subjects. While certainly relevant to courses in statistics, it is at least as important in courses that attract those students who are data challenged, who tilt toward verbal and visual skills, but who are likely to be making organizational decisions at all levels in government, nonprofits, and the private sector. Graduates who have avoided quantitative courses for fear of failure may find themselves, decades later, running large educational or arts organizations, or even at the helm of multi-billion-dollar government or private entities. They will need to understand and to utilize data rather than simply delegate it to specialized staff.

The authors have accomplished a significant public service by presenting a pathway for data literacy, especially in an emerging era of data analytics and AI. Over the course of their careers, any reader of this volume will find themselves more comfortable with data and perceived by others as more competent in making data-driven decisions. It is a small investment with a high payoff for individuals, their present or future organizations, and the citizens they serve.

McIntyre-Lahner and Schack have presented us with a book that offers a bridge from fear to function. It is a necessary complement to courses on statistics or quantitative decision-making and should become widely adopted in public administration, public policy, and nonprofit programs, as well as many professional degrees. Because we all need to be prepared to manage and lead organizations, we all need to overcome our misunderstandings and fears of data so that we might expertly participate in a data-informed culture.

Marc Holzer, Ph.D.
Founding Dean and Professor Emeritus, School of Public Affairs and Administration, Rutgers University
Founder, National Center for Public Performance
Feb. 13, 2024

Acknowledgements

The authors would like to acknowledge their families for their support and encouragement; Marc Holzer; Mohamad Alkadry and colleagues at the UCONN School of Public Policy; Lisa Schack for her technical assistance and infinite patience; Liz Lahner for the fear monster illustrations; Carolann Schack for the cave painting illustrations; Mark and Olivia Lahner for holding down the farm so we could write; Mark Friedman; Barry Goff; Bennett Pudlin; Meg Streams; William Carbone; Toni Harp; Chris Marcelli; Morgan Considine; Sherry Haller; Jim Boucher; Janice Gruendel; Lyle Wray in memoriam; Adam Luecking and the Clear Impact team; UCONN School of Public Policy interns; and the many colleagues who have helped us grow in our data work over the years.

Introduction

Both authors of this book are data consultants, teachers, and former government employees. In these various roles, we have encountered, and continue to encounter, data fear in its many manifestations. Having worked together on many projects over the years, we often discussed data fear and how it can be a real barrier to progress on data projects and how we have seen these data fears overcome. Back in 2018, we presented some of our initial thinking on the topic at the National Public Performance Conference at Suffolk University. This presentation was very well received, and we began to more fully develop these ideas in the months and years that followed. Our intent in writing this book is to present these ideas so that they would be useful to a wide audience, both those suffering from data fear and those who may be comfortable with data but would like to help their students, colleagues, and others overcome data fear and add value to their data projects, organizations, and communities.

It is important to note that this book is NOT about "how to become a data scientist" or other kind of technical data wizard. We encourage anyone interested in pursuing more advanced data analytic work to do so, but that is not the emphasis of this book. This book is about data fear, and how to overcome it, so that those facing data fear can become more comfortable with data, more effectively engage with data, and not allow data fear to create a barrier to using data to understand the world, solve problems, and make a difference in their organizations.

Some of our colleagues write and teach about data literacy… we applaud and support that. However, we believe that if individuals are afraid of data – afraid of their lack of current skills, or lack of ability; afraid of how data will be used to measure their work; afraid of the implications that measurement will have on

DOI: 10.4324/9781003496328-1

their programs, organizations and careers – they will not be in a position to learn about data and to be able to engage in and progress along the generally recognized steps of data literacy: understanding data; using data; analyzing data; and arguing with data. A first step in achieving data literacy is addressing and overcoming data fear. If you want to add value to your organization through the use of data, you must face these fears and start your journey towards data-comfort.

We began our work on this subject to provide a resource for practitioners in the social services and related fields; those practitioners who are hampered by data fear and those who seek to empower colleagues hampered by data fear. As we developed approaches to assist individuals with data fear, it became clear to us, that data fear also affects groups of individuals and can become pervasive in some organizations. After many hours of field work and reflection, we came to understand that data fear impacts and inhibits many different groups of individuals as well as organizations, organizational networks, and communities.[1] We believe in order to address data fear in organizations, it is necessary to also address data fear on an individual level within those organizations.

Fear and anxiety about data, both internally oriented, and externally oriented, deter some potentially key partners from participating in measurement, evaluation, and other data-related efforts. Our work with nonprofit and government organizations over many years has afforded us the opportunity to encounter, understand, and categorize these fears and to identify actions that both individuals and organizational leaders can take in order to alleviate the anxiety so that more colleagues, community members, and other potential partners are willing to actively participate in data-related efforts.

This book is intended for multiple audiences, from students making their first forays into data work, to practitioners who have struggled with data in the past, to savvy data people who want to help others transcend their data fear. While this book begins with a focus on data fear in individuals, we later explore data fear at the organizational, collaborative, and community levels. As such, this book is also appropriate for those who may experience data fear in any of those contexts.

In this book, we will:

◆ Describe different types and degrees of data fear (a data fear/data comfort continuum)
◆ Discuss how those who are comfortable with and use data regularly–and particularly "data professionals," sometimes amplify data fear in others
◆ Provide a self-assessment instrument and process to help individuals assess their level of data fear/comfort, and identify which dimensions of data fear/comfort may be problematic for them
◆ Revisit that same assessment with an organizational lens as we later discuss data fear in organizations; and also in networks, and communities
◆ Articulate an overall approach to "managing data fear"
◆ Provide a tool-box of fear-fighting techniques, including methods of dealing with data fear "in the moment," methods of mitigating data fear related to using, sharing, and reporting data, and demonstrating how many common data tasks need not be scary.
◆ Discuss how to "bake in" data fear prevention into your efforts to create and sustain a data informed culture.

Whatever your level of data comfort, we hope this book provides some additional understanding, insight, and strategies that you can apply either to transcend your own data fears or help others to do so.

Note

1 We are especially grateful to Marc Holzer for his support, guidance, and willingness to share resources and ideas.

Part I

The Nature of Data Fear

1

The Nature of Fear

When Anne was a kid, she was convinced that monsters really were under the bed. The monster of the evening could vary (Dracula, Frankenstein's monster), but she was convinced something was under the bed, and she used to take a running leap to avoid being grasped by the ankle and pulled under the bed into the scary darkness and being exposed to whatever terrible things happened when monsters grab the ankles of unsuspecting kids. She also jumped into bed with the light still on (because monsters only existed in the dark) and made sure her bedroom door was open (because if someone else was in hearing distance, the monster couldn't get her). In other words, she did everything within her power to avoid a confrontation with the monster under the bed (Figure 1.1).

When we write about the "Data Fear Monster" and how that monster impacts the careers of hard-working students and professionals, we are talking about a very similar kind of fear. The feelings we have as those fears manifest themselves lead to negative behaviors; these negative behaviors tend to reinforce our fears. A monstrous cycle, to be sure.

We define **the data fear monster** as the manifestation of fear feelings, including a lurking dread related to data, that lead to a range of thoughts and behaviors, including **paralysis** of thought; **avoidance** of use, which reinforces beliefs and behaviors about one's lack of ability or distrust of data use by others; or **dismissal or denial** of the importance of data, leading to lack of engagement with, and use of, data. These elements are part of a

DOI: 10.4324/9781003496328-3

FIGURE 1.1 Scary data fear monster.
Source: Liz Lahner drawnbyeal.com.

self-defeating cycle that allows the fear to feed on itself, generally causing the fear to grow.

The fear monster can be experienced differently by each person, in both the type and depth of the fear response. The depth of the fear response may cause a variety of responses from

FIGURE 1.2 Three fear monsters.
Source: Liz Lahner drawnbyeal.com.

refusing to work with data to suffering from imposter syndrome when working on data-related tasks.

It is possible to overcome data fear and to vanquish the data fear monster – the data fear monster responds to confrontation the way most real and imagined bullies do; it may not disappear, but it shrinks in importance, power, and scariness. This is because the data fear monster works in a very specific way: its power comes from the fear itself. Our own fear. The fear inside us. *Specifically, the fear that our perceived shortcomings will cause us to fail at the task is the power behind the fear monster; and the way to overcome the fear is to confront those fears and either vanquish the monster or be vanquished by it.* Once we engage the data fear monster and begin to grapple with our disempowering beliefs and actions, we begin to identify the specific characteristics of the monster and the specific ways it shows up within us. In short, when we begin to identify and understand how the fear monster works within us, we take the first steps in freeing ourselves from the fear monster (Figure 1.3).

FIGURE 1.3 Vanquished fear monster.
Source: Liz Lahner drawnbyeal.com.

The data fear monster may never go away completely for some of us; however, we can transform our relationship with it by using the tools described in this book to understand, address, and manage our fears related to data use.

Avoidance does the job of shielding scared kids from imaginary monsters under the bed, but at a cost – and only on a temporary basis. Anne never knew for sure that the monster wasn't there, just waiting for her, and if she needed to get up in the middle of the night, she had to go through the whole routine again to continue with her avoidance strategy (Figure 1.4).

Similarly, avoidance can shield the working professional – but also at a cost, and only for a time.

Avoiding working with data can give the impression of being protected from the fear monster. In reality, however, all it does is allow an individual to ignore information that is either potentially useful, and should be investigated or utilized, or is potentially damaging, and should be addressed. By saying things like

FIGURE 1.4 Toolbox fear monster.
Source: Liz Lahner drawnbyeal.com.

FIGURE 1.5 Monster with heart.
Source: Liz Lahner drawnbyeal.com.

"I don't do data" or "I don't have a brain for that," we can create a false belief that it is ok to ignore or abdicate a portion of the work (Figure 1.5).

Moving Toward the Fear

In Part III of this book, we will be sharing a "fear fighting toolbox" – a collection of strategies to help fight and tame the data fear monster. In order to use these tools effectively, it is important that, rather than avoiding data fear, working professionals move toward the fear – understanding the sources, types, and nature of data fear. The first part of this book explores data fear in its various manifestations and provides a foundation for the use of the collection of tools in the fear-fighting toolbox. Part II of this book will help you assess and understand where you are on the data fear/data comfort continuum and identify areas that you can address using the fear-fighting toolbox in Part III.

First Things First... What Do We Mean by Data?

Data, of course, come in many forms, both qualitative and quantitative. Quantitative data are information about quantities and therefore numbers, and qualitative data are descriptive, and regards phenomenon which can be observed but not measured, such as language.[1] So basically, quantitative data are the numbers and qualitative data are the pictures, explanations, and narratives that reveal information that the numbers alone may not.

When you type the word "data" into that all-knowing search engine, Google, the first definition provided[2] is "facts and statistics collected together for reference or analysis"...the same site goes on to provide two other definitions:

"the quantities, characters, or symbols on which operations are performed by a computer, being stored and transmitted in the form of electrical signals and recorded on magnetic, optical, or mechanical recording media" and things known or assumed as facts, making the basis of reasoning or calculation.

These are very rich definitions...the first emphasizes "facts collected together," while the second is more granular...the "individual quantities...on which operations are performed." The third emphasizes data as "the basis of reasoning or calculation." These are appropriately very general definitions of data. For purposes of this book, we use the term data to include **any observations, either qualitative or quantitative used to help us understand the universe – in particular, information that we compile, analyze, and report to help us understand what is happening in our organizations, our systems, and communities.** We also use data to help us understand demographic, economic, and environmental factors, as well as the *performance* of organizations, systems, and programs.

For those who may feel overwhelmed when faced with a bunch of numbers, it may help to remember that "Data" is a plural noun; the singular of data is "datum," "a piece of information; an assumption or premise from which inferences may be drawn; and/or a fixed starting point of a scale or operation,"[3] or "a single point of information."[4] Thinking about a single piece of information may be less intimidating and may create an opportunity to begin thinking about data in a non-threatening way.

While we focus on numerical information, we will also discuss how qualitative information contextualizes numerical data and can be used to assist our colleagues in thinking about data as approachable.

Data Meditation: Counting and Categorizing

Sometimes it is easy to forget that fundamentally, working with data starts with COUNTING THINGS. Before we get to calculating measures, doing comparisons, or determining whether the differences we see are meaningful, we start with counting things…the frequency with which things occur…the number of activities, people, things produced, and outcomes achieved. We often also CATEGORIZE the things that we count, to help us understand better what we are counting.

Such counting and categorizing are foundational to the human experience. Even Neanderthals counted and categorized things. Consider the following (Figure 1.6):

Animal	Number of Times Seen	Number of Times Eaten
	IIII	II
	HHII IIII	IIII
	IIII	I
Totals	17	7

FIGURE 1.6 Neanderthal chart.
Source: Created by the authors.

You could imagine some intrepid Neanderthals counting creatures they have encountered, and successfully hunted and eaten, on their cave wall. Take a minute to think about the insight even these simple counts provide before you continue reading.

These simple counts might tell our Neanderthals:

♦ How often they are likely to see different kinds of prey
♦ Unless they do something different, how often they will successfully hunt and eat different kinds of prey
♦ What approximate proportion of their meat intake comes from what kind of prey
♦ And, in the case of the giant sloth, the lack of consumption points to the likelihood they don't like the taste ☺

As you can see, simple counting and categorizing can provide a great deal of insight. Imagine in our fantasy Neanderland that aliens have recently provided them with a laptop computer. They could decide to increase the sophistication of their data analysis using the alien version of Microsoft Excel, after gathering some more data (Table 1.1).

Spreadsheets can be scary, but they really are not all that different from the cave diagram...what can be seen when the Neanderthals additional data collection is examined? How do the seasons affect what is seen and eaten?

Of course, other creatures may use counting and categorizing too. A hungry Smilodon might use Excel to build the following chart (Figure 1.7):

Moving from simple counts to a spreadsheet to a chart is really a basic process and should not instill fear for long. Just remember, we all count things, and working with data starts with counting!

So why do some people fear data? Let's face it – for some people it is the numbers and associated analysis, calculation, and advanced statistics that people fear – not the information itself or what it might tell them. These people are afraid to engage with data due to their real or perceived lack of skills, lack of understanding of mathematical and statistical processes, and self-perceived lack of ability. For others, data fear is related to how the information

TABLE 1.1 Neanderthal Excel Chart

	Spring		Summer		Fall		Winter		Total		Percent Eaten of Those Seen
	Seen	Eaten	Seen	Eaten	Seen	Eaten	Seen	Eaten	Seen	Eaten	
Mammoth	30	6	24	4	28	5	36	12	118	27	22.9%
Bison	42	18	49	21	34	18	14	8	139	65	46.8%
Sloth	8	1	12	0	10	0	9	3	39	4	10.3%
Bear	5	1	6	2	8	3	12	4	31	10	32.3%
Totals	85	26	91	27	80	26	71	27	327	106	32.4%

Source: Created by the authors

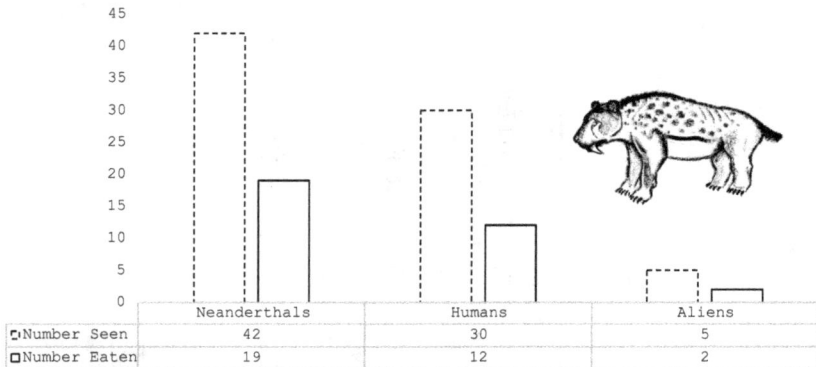

	Neanderthals	Humans	Aliens
◻ Number Seen	42	30	5
◻ Number Eaten	19	12	2

FIGURE 1.7 Smilodon snack chart.
Source: Created by the authors.

could be used. Specifically, they fear what could happen to the data once it is released: misinterpretation, over-generalization, incorrect assumptions, or erroneous conclusions. These could lead to cuts in funding, firings, program closures, or embarrassment and shame for the disseminator of the data. Further, as we will describe, the two types of fears sometimes combine to create a bigger problem: fear about lack of ability combines with fear about how much effort it will take to generate something useful and is compounded by fear about how any reported data might be used that scares people. And in many ways, what this book boils down to is transcending those fears and being able to comprehend and use information to understand our world and make good decisions.

We all know fear. Of course, not all fear is created equal… there is a continuum of fear, from a slight qualm or uneasiness to crippling fear that renders us unable to take any action at all. As Frank Herbert wrote in his classic science-fiction novel, Dune, "Fear is the mind-killer…. fear is the little death that leads to total obliteration."

On the other hand, fear can be useful…nature hasn't selected out our capacity for fear because fear, in some circumstances, provides us with important signals about our environment that we should act on…like the fear we feel when we sense someone is following us, or the fear we feel before we eat food that might be spoiled.

Often, however, the level of fear we feel is not proportional to the threat – either perceived or real. It may prevent us from acting when some action is necessary, or create a debilitating degree of caution that causes us to postpone decisions or choose something else to do rather than engage with the perceived threat. In other words, it is the fear itself that holds us back, not necessarily the actual task. Sometimes that fear protects us, but other times it just holds us back from doing something important.

In reviewing the "fear" literature, we were struck with the commonalities woven throughout. Most importantly, the authors we reviewed agree fear can be overcome; we don't have to be controlled by our fears. We were also struck by the somewhat different characterizations of fear and our relationship to fear. For example, one author, Russ Harris, contends that "the *actions* of confidence come first, the *feelings* of confidence come later" and cites five reasons why people lack confidence: excessive expectations, harsh self-judgment, pre-occupation with fear, lack of experience, and lack of skill.[5] Another author, Stephen Hayes, notes several important myths about fear, including (1) fear is a sign of weakness, (2) fear impairs performance, (3) fear holds you back [he contends it is not fear that holds you back – it is your attitude toward it that keeps you stuck], and (4) confidence is the absence of fear [he notes genuine confidence is not the absence of fear – it is the *transformed relationship* with fear].[6]

Some authors emphasize the basic and primal nature of our core fears. Jeffrey Pressman contends that that there are five core FEARS – (1) abandonment (loss of love), (2) loss of identity, (3) loss of meaning, (4) loss of purpose (the chance to express oneself fully), and (5)…the big kahuna…DEATH (including fear of pain and sickness that might lead to death). He argues that we create counterproductive defenses that are intended to protect ourselves from our core fears, and that these defenses backfire, tending to "cause the problem they were designed to fix."' For Pressman, "the master key to resolving fear is doing the opposite of the chief defense."[7]

Aligned with Pressman's emphasis on the five core fears, Thich Nhat Hahn writes of the "five remembrances" – including growing old, ill health, dying, loss of what you love, and the fact that one inherits their acts of body, speech, and mind. Seems like kind of a bummer...quite a bit of existential angst ☺. But Hahn argues that the practice of the five remembrances help us accept many of our deepest fears – such as old age, sickness, and death – as realities, facts we cannot escape. When we practice accepting these truths, we *realize peace and have the capacity to live conscious, healthy, and compassionate lives, no longer causing suffering to ourselves and others.*[8] This at first blush seems rather far afield from data fear, but it really isn't. Data fear *can* be triggered by, or associated with, more deep-seated fears related to abandonment, loss of identity, loss of meaning, loss of purpose, and, as Hahn so eloquently emphasizes, change and death. As we quoted from Frank Herbert's *Dune* earlier in the book...."fear is the *little death*," paradoxically robbing us of our capacity to live our lives fully. A big part of Hahn's recipe for combating fear – even the deep-seated core fears referenced above – is mindfulness. We have several exercises in Part III of the book, starting with **Anne's Anxiety Buster** that rely on the principles of mindfulness, which we will discuss in more detail as we describe these strategies.

Something we have seen often, in ourselves and others, is the fear of being embarrassed because either we don't know, or can't do, something related to data. When unpacked, this fear of embarrassment may also be something much more complicated. Ron has come to understand that a part of this fear of embarrassment was related to a fear of himself...how he would see himself and how he would treat himself when such embarrassment was suffered. This self-shame, and the attempted avoidance of it, can get you stuck on the data comfort continuum in the areas of data dread, data avoidance, and even data paralysis. It can also pop up later, when you are more generally comfortable with data, as imposter syndrome. The fear of being "found out" as being less data savvy than you are perceived to be is a form of this fear of embarrassment and the self-shame that might result. The fear that many individuals experience regarding data is both disproportionate and learned. We learn to fear data when it is taught poorly, and we don't have the requisite information to understand concepts being taught; when we have negative experiences using data; and when we experience data being used incorrectly and punitively. These "learned" data fears can serve as a catalyst for the activation of the deeper, core fears discussed earlier, amplifying the associated feelings of fear and making facing them even more daunting. In other words, poor teaching can activate and/or intensify our already pre-existing core fears.

In this book, we will explore how data fear is manifested, and we will provide opportunities to overcome data fear. We will also examine how disproportionate fear of data can be a self-fulfilling prophesy – "I can't; therefore, I don't" – and how that can also be overcome

We categorize the two main types of data fear as:

◆ Fear Related to Your Own Lack of Capacity or Lack of Skill(s)
◆ Fear Related to How Data Will Be Used

When we write about fear related to lack of capacity, we are writing about both fear stemming from our belief that we may not be able to understand or learn a particular technique, and also fear emanating from our knowledge that we do not possess particular data skills that should be applied to a data task we are confronted with.

But there is another whole category of fear, fear of data related to how that data will be used. Data fear related to use includes fear of loss of control, weaponization of data, fear of being embarrassed by data, fear of data being misinterpreted, and fear of violating rules related to sharing data. We discuss this type of data fear in a later chapter.

There is a strong interplay between the two types: individuals who doubt their own skills or have weak or undeveloped data skills are more likely to distrust data in general and will be more likely to distrust what others will do with data. Further, because they don't understand some of the mathematical processes – what they mean, their limitations, and also their benefits – they are less likely to understand those benefits and the importance of being able to qualify, or contextualize, what the data do and do not tell us. When sharing data, the qualifications and limitations are important to understand and be able to include as part of a responsible, empowering, and effective data sharing effort. When someone believes they don't fully understand the limitations and how to qualify the data, they will likely be less willing to share it.

There are times when fear about our lack of ability combines with fear related to use, and packs a double wallop, convincing us even more strongly that we don't have the ability to do the work, or the skills to correct its misuse once it leaves our control. For those of us who are susceptible to both types of data fear, this double whammy works by engaging both types of data fear at the same time, causing each type of fear to amplify the other. An individual who doubts her own data skills, and who is required to provide data-related information to another individual or organization, is likely to feel intimidated by preparing, ana- lyzing, or producing that information. Believing that the infor- mation may be misused or misinterpreted, and that she doesn't have the skills to counter the misuse or misinterpretation, may lead to increased feelings of fear:

> I'm not sure I can do this, or that I can do it correctly; and I'm worried that someone is going to misunderstand the data, or will misuse it….AND I don't have the ability to either help them understand the data, to correct a misinterpretation, or to refute a misuse of the data.

Throughout the book, we identify behaviors and responses related to the different types of data fear; these behaviors can be better understood as *manifestations* of data fear. More specific- ally, data fear manifests itself as feelings, and related behaviors, associated with using data. These fear-based feelings range from extreme, paralyzing fear, to a sense of discomfort and lack of con- fidence about working with data. The behaviors that accompany these feelings range from total avoidance, to minimizing and discrediting the importance of data, to a reluctant agreement to use data. When we refer to the data fear monster, we are referring to the impact of data fear and how that fear manifests itself in the types of feelings and behaviors described above. We are very familiar with roots of data fear, having experienced it ourselves and seen it manifest itself in others throughout our careers and even in our developmental years.

While very comfortable with data now, Ron was NOT comfortable with data in elementary school and high school. He didn't like being asked to do long division at the blackboard and developed "performance anxiety." This anxiety became associated with math, and Ron soon decided he didn't like math because of that. This dislike of math carried over into high school, and because he "didn't like it," he didn't work very hard in his math classes. It wasn't until graduate school that Ron started to feel like he both really needed and appreciated math. It took some doing, but he became convinced he could do advanced math, and eventually took several advanced math and statistics classes. Armed with this new appreciation of math and data analysis, Ron brought this new confidence in his own abilities to his job as the performance measurement coordinator at the Connecticut Department of Labor (CTDOL). The performance measurement unit produced reports of unemployment insurance and employment service data for each of CTDOL's 18 job centers. It was Ron's job to go out to each job center to review the center's performance with the staff. He immediately encountered data fear with many staff members, who resisted talking about the numbers. They felt overwhelmed, defensive, and misunderstood. Their first instinct was to question the data – and usually not with the intention of making things better – but rather with the intention of "making the whole thing go away." CTDOL decided that data training was need for job center staff. Ron conducted this training, too, and he encountered a lot of data fear, especially around concepts like "the normal distribution," "standard deviation," and "statistical significance." Some was run of the mill resistance – "we don't really need this training," "we will never really use this training" – but some was more related to being asked to look at numbers at all and being asked to make choices based on data.

Anne's story has a lot in common with Ron's story. Anne did pretty well with math throughout elementary and middle school. It wasn't her favorite subject, but she understood the topics and did well enough. However, once she got to high school and encountered algebra and geometry and had to start using formulas to solve equations, she began to struggle. It seemed as if each lesson built on the last one, so the further into each semester she traveled, the more behind she got, and the more lost she felt.

Due to a series of family moves, Anne attended three high schools, and with each move, she experienced a lack of continuity in the educational experience. For most topics, that was fine; but mathematics became a bigger problem and gave Anne the opportunity to slip out of the educational track she had been in for math and enroll in less and less challenging classes where she could just get by. She started to describe herself as stupid in math.

In college, Anne was able to focus on the courses she enjoyed – languages, writing, and psychology – and minimize her involvement with math and data-related topics for the first couple of semesters.

This was before she encountered the concept of "data" as something she might need to use in her personal and professional life; any concept of "data" was relegated to distant memories of high school science, and the "math-y" side of psychology, which she did not feel called to pursue at that time.

During one college summer, in the days of adding machines and hand calculations, Anne worked as a cost-accounting clerk. She was surprised to learn that she was actually pretty good at basic accounting tasks using the math skills she didn't believe she possessed.

However, it wasn't for another decade that Anne would have her first epiphany about the use of data to inform policy and performance, and how incredibly important it is:

I remember exactly where I was when the numbers started jumping off the page! I was reading the first report created about the demographic information on adolescents referred to the state's juvenile justice system, and it became really clear, really fast, that different groups of kids were treated differently. All of a sudden, stories that the kids had told me started to make sense, and I had questions that needed answers.

Over the next 20+ years, Anne embraced the use of data and the power it could bring to understanding current practice, and measuring both the need for change, and the system's success at implementing change efforts. Like Ron, she found that many of her colleagues were unwilling to embrace the use of data in their work, and were suspicious of concepts they didn't fully understand, or that they perceived might be used to judge them. Her work developed to the point where she was asked to lead the effort in moving her agency from one that measured success by anecdotes, to an agency that used data to measure and manage performance. Again, like Ron, she encountered resistance on the part of colleagues, and outright refusal by some, to use data. People were afraid of using data; some were afraid their lack of skills would call them out as ignorant or unintelligent, while others were afraid of how outsiders would misinterpret the data and judge their work.

We know that data fear exists, and we understand the fear can have a crippling effect on those in its grip. We also know that data fear can be replaced by varying degrees of comfort with understanding and using data.

Understanding the roots of data fear can help us develop strategies for dealing with that fear. When such fear is encountered, it is helpful to recognize that it can be deep-seated, developed early on in life, and as such not easily set aside or eradicated. Even when we succeed in transcending data fear, it can linger on, re-appearing when a particularly difficult data task (or threat) appears. The roots of data fear can be very personal, stemming from particularly difficult episodes of data struggle. This can also be self-fulfilling, for early experiences can "taint" future attempts to re-engage with data, dooming those attempts to at worst, fail, and best, to be unpleasant, and therefore unlikely to be attempted again. However, having an awareness of the roots of data fear, and being mindful of them, is a first step on the path to overcoming them.

Part of our thesis is that you need to be data literate in order to be truly data comfortable and that you need to be comfortable using data to be truly literate; *however, simply emphasizing skill building is often not enough;* acknowledging and understanding the sources of data fear is often necessary in order to address, and overcome, that fear. Similarly, being comfortable with data does not ensure that one is data literate. As Adam Grant points out in his book, *Think Again*, being confident in one's ability does not ensure accuracy. Experiments have shown that as one acquires skills, confidence can far outpace accuracy and understanding. Grant argues that what we need is confident humility...having faith in our capability while appreciating we might not have the right solution.[9]

Acknowledging and understanding the sources of data fear can help to break down barriers to embarking upon, or effectively gaining, data skills. Without such acknowledgement and understanding, some people suffering from data fear may never reach the point where they feel ready to engage with data. And just because someone becomes comfortable with data – "oh yeah, I can just whip that into Excel and generate this pretty chart... piece of cake," – doesn't mean they are actually data literate and have learned what they need to know in order to engage with data in valid and legitimate ways.

Data Literacy

For our purposes, we use the MIT definition of data literacy[10,11], which includes the ability to read, work with, analyze, and argue with data. Reading data involves understanding what data are and what aspects of the world it represents. This includes being able to read and understand data reports. It includes making the connection between numbers on a page and the real-life concepts, actions, and conditions they represent. Reading data means being able to understand what the data are telling us and the conclusions that can, and – equally important – cannot be made from data as reported.

Working with data involves creating, acquiring, cleaning, and managing it. When we refer to data cleaning, we do not mean buffing the data with a fine chamois; rather, we mean looking at the data for duplicate entries, inconsistent data labeling, or data that have inappropriately shifted from one column to another and other similar issues. Creating data involves making observations and collecting and recording those observations. This can mean taking notes, collecting images, counting things, collecting responses to surveys, etc. Acquiring data means getting data from other places, such as businesses, administrative agencies, or even the Internet. Once you have these data, either data you collect or data you acquire, they need to be review for quality, cleaned up, and then put into a usable format and managed over time.

Analyzing data involves filtering, sorting, aggregating, comparing, and performing other such analytic operations on it. This is where the data often come to life and begin to tell their story. It can be the "slicing and dicing," aggregating, or disaggregating that allows us to really understand the story behind the numbers. Analyzing also includes looking at one set of data compared to another – or maybe many others. (See the analysis section in Part III of our book – *Analysis Doesn't Have To Be Scary* for more on analyzing data.) Not everyone needs to be able to perform all analyses; however, it is important to understand the concepts behind some of the more involved or sophisticated analyses and to understand when they are called for and why.

Arguing with data involves using data to support a larger narrative intended to communicate some message to a particular audience. It requires us to have a deep-enough understanding of what the data represent, what the analyses show, and how the information and analyses support the questions, assertions, and conclusions we put forth in our data-based arguments.

Notes

1 https://www.simplypsychology.org/qualitative-quantitative.html.
2 https://www.lexico.com/en/definition/data.
3 As retrieved from https://www.lexico.com/en/definition/data.
4 As retrieved from https://dictionary.cambridge.org/us/dictionary/english/datum.
5 Harris, Russ, *The Confidence Gap: A Guide to Overcoming Fear and Self Doubt*. Boulder, CO: Trumpeter Books, 2011.

6 See *Acceptance and Commitment Therapy: An Experiential Approach to Behavior Change* by Stephen Hayes.

7 Pressman, Todd, *Deconstructing Anxiety: The Journey from Fear to Fulfillment*. Lanham, MD: Rowman and Littlefield, 2019.

8 Nhat Hahn, Thich. *Fear: Essential Wisdom for Getting Through the Storm*. New York: Harper Collins, 2012.

9 Grant, Adam, *Think Again*. Viking: New York, 2021.

10 Bhargava, R., & D'Ignazio, C. (2015). Designing tools and activities for data literacy learners. In *Wed Science: Data Literacy Workshop*. Oxford, UK.

11 D'Ignazio, C., & Bhargava, R. (2016). DataBasic: Design principles, tools and activities for data literacy learners. *The Journal of Community Informatics,* 12(3).

2

Stages of Data Comfort

In this next section, we move beyond a discussion of data literacy to examining different stages of comfort with data. We have commented that many of our colleagues are focused on data literacy, and that this book focuses on overcoming data fear and getting to data comfort. You may wonder what the difference is between data literacy and data comfort, and be tempted to see them as the same thing. We expect that if a person is competent at something, they will be comfortable doing it; and if someone is comfortable doing something, they are competent at it – right? And when we look at lack of comfort and lack of competence, we might expect that people who are not competent at something are also not comfortable with it; and people who are not comfortable doing a particular type of work will not be good at it.

Actually, that is not necessarily the case; and understanding this is a continuum and language that isn't redundant but introduces the reader to us exploring the comfort-competence continuum further.

We have invested years in understanding what we refer to as the convergence of comfort and competence (including data literacy). More importantly, our work also includes identifying the difference between comfort and competence, why it matters, how these two factors are related, and how we can use our understanding of the relationship to increase your competence and comfort so that you can overcome your data fear and begin to confidently work with data.

DOI: 10.4324/9781003496328-4

In many instances, the convergence of comfort and competence is strong; people who are good at something are often comfortable with it; and when people are comfortable with certain tasks, they are also often good at those tasks. However, that is not always true. There are plenty of people who are comfortable in their role, but are certainly not competent at it. This is known as the Dunning-Kruger effect: The Dunning-Kruger effect is a cognitive bias in which people wrongly overestimate their knowledge or ability in a specific area. This tends to occur because a lack of self-awareness prevents them from accurately assessing their own skills.[1]

Consider the following examples:

♦ Self-proclaimed experts – some who actually "know everything" - who love to enlighten others, and unfortunately display their lack of competence the more they speak
♦ Consulting an authority who exudes confidence about a specific topic, only to find out you know more than they do
♦ Hiring a "let the experts handle this" kind of technician to fix something, and realizing your attempt at fixing it worked better
♦ Coworkers who have held their positions for many years, without updating their skills, and consequently are very comfortable at their jobs, but do not perform their work in accordance with best practices or current standards

Likewise, some people are highly competent at a task or job, but lack the confidence in their skills or ability to feel comfortable being characterized as an expert. This dissonance between skill and confidence is known as Imposter Syndrome[2], and we will revisit Imposter Syndrome later in this section. Examples of Imposter Syndrome include

♦ An introvert who is an excellent teacher and highly skilled in a subject, but is not comfortable speaking to groups and doesn't feel they can do a good job teaching others

◆ A gifted singer or musician who doubts her talents and is afraid to perform

◆ A coworker with strong systems knowledge, but who doubts himself and must be continually nudged to share his insights in the planning or other discussions

◆ A recognized expert who still experiences doubt periodically— "who am I to be making this speech?" "What business do I have teaching this class"

It is clear that competence and comfort do not always go together[3]. Our work has taught us two important things about the relationship between competence and comfort:

1. It is possible to move past data fear, and begin to work with data – no matter how uncomfortable it is at first; and

2. For someone who fears data, and doubts their ability to work with data, learning how to get past their fear and discomfort helps immensely in beginning to develop competence, and eventually well-founded confidence in the ability to do the work.

Continuum of Data Fear/Comfort

We believe there is a continuum of data fear and data comfort. On the extreme end of the "fear" side of the continuum are fear states like data dread and data paralysis…fear that is so overwhelming that no data-related actions take place. On the extreme end of the "comfort" side of the continuum are "comfort states" like data empowerment and data advocacy…where teaching, mentoring, and sharing about data come naturally.

The following "Continuum of Data Comfort" shows a natural progression from the most extreme kinds of data fear to states of fully developed data comfort. As suggested above, dealing with these fears about data will set the stage for the acquisition of data skills and foster data literacy. It is important to note that while we have depicted this as a linear continuum, there can be moments when people regress to earlier fear states momentarily, due to the nature of the data task they face. And, even regular data users can experience data fear and doubt, particularly when making transitions to new tools, methodologies, or data-use settings. However, this comfort continuum is intended to represent how most of us who experience data fear progressively work through these challenges.

In the table, we have labeled different points on the comfort continuum, and assigned each a certain fear level. We then describe the "fear feelings" associated with each fear level, and the associated behaviors that flow from those feelings. We also briefly describe the developmental challenges associated with each point on the continuum.

It is important to note that while we are representing the comfort continuum as linear, actual experience may not be like this. Even when someone is generally comfortable with data tasks, they can experience fear feelings that are further back on the continuum. Depending on the task, circumstances, and current feeling or state, it is possible to experience multiple states on the continuum at the same time.

Later in the book, we will describe how to manage these fear feelings and behaviors. For now, it is important to understand the data fear/data comfort continuum, the kinds of fear feelings that can be experienced, and that it is possible to transcend those fears and progress along the continuum (Table 2.1).

Points On the Continuum

The Data Fear-Comfort Continuum

The Data Fear-Comfort Continuum has two states grounded in data fear, a neutral state that represents the beginning of a crossover to a state of data comfort, and two states representing different levels of data comfort. The states are described below and plotted out on the accompanying chart. Finding where you sit on the continuum can be a first step to changing that place and moving toward data comfort.

TABLE 2.1 Comfort-Fear Continuum

Data Fear-Comfort Level	Expression of Fear or Comfort	Fear or Comfort Feelings	Behaviors Related to Fear or Comfort about One's Capacity	Behaviors Related to Fear or Comfort of Use of Data	Developmental Task	Fear-Fighting Tool
Data Dread/Paralysis	FEAR	You feel terror and can be paralyzed at the thought of having to incorporate data in your work in any way; it stops you in your tracks, giving you that "deer in headlights" feeling	Total Avoidance of using data; you "know," and often state, that you just can't "do data," and try to change the subject or focus on other important facets of the work	You avoid data use and reporting requirements, and focus on anecdotal information and relationships; you don't even consider sharing data so that others can't "use it against" your organization or program, or create data questions you can't answer	Understand your fear and its genesis; consider that you may be able to change, and that it may be possible for you to understand and use basic data	Review Anne's Anxiety Buster and Ron's Anxiety Buster; create your own Anxiety Buster and practice with it to get comfortable in data-related situations
Data Dismissal/Avoidance	FEAR	You fear that you are unable to develop the skills to use data, and if data use is required in your job, you fear you don't have the ability to work with data, or to manage how data-based reports are interpreted and used by others	You dismiss the use of data as overrated and time-wasting, taking away from more important work, and avoid using data, prioritizing other tasks over data tasks	You focus on "doing the actual work" and dismiss sharing data as time-wasting or potentially compromising client or constituent privacy; You avoid reporting and using data so that it can't be incorrectly interpreted or used by others without your ability to correct it	Rise above your fears enough that you can imagine how data might be beneficial to the work Start to pay attention to how data is being used, and learn the techniques to calm your feelings of anxiety when thinking about data	Employ your anxiety buster Read the "Counting and Categorizing" and "Three Things You Can See" Data Meditations, and consider how you do, or could, use the concepts they describe

(Continued)

TABLE 2.1 (Continued) Comfort-Fear Continuum

Data Fear-Comfort Level	Expression of Fear or Comfort	Fear or Comfort Feelings	Behaviors Related to Fear or Comfort about One's Capacity	Behaviors Related to Fear or Comfort of Use of Data	Developmental Task	Fear-Fighting Tool
Data Doubt – Acquiescence	NEUTRAL/ CROSSOVER	You realize that data are not going away, even though you continue to have doubt about your ability; you accept that it is worthwhile to consider using data, but still feel intimidated at the thought of engaging with data work	you may reluctantly engage in some limited data tasks, but you continue to express and feel doubt about your ability to do the work	While you don't trust how others will interpret your data, and your ability to counter any resulting issues, you begin to release data on a limited basis	Begin using data with support and coaching; explore and challenge your doubts and find a trusted source to help you understand more complex data questions and methods	Identify a trusted data mentor or coach you can utilize as an ongoing resource; Review "Analysis Doesn't need to be Scary" and take its step-by-step approach to addressing one data task you have been avoiding. Employ your anxiety buster if you feel overwhelmed

(Continued)

TABLE 2.1 (Continued) Comfort-Fear Continuum

Data Fear-Comfort Level	Expression of Fear or Comfort	Fear or Comfort Feelings	Behaviors Related to Fear or Comfort about One's Capacity	Behaviors Related to Fear or Comfort of Use of Data	Developmental Task	Fear-Fighting Tool
Data Embrace	COMFORT	You begin to experience some level of comfort at the thought of using data and find yourself starting to enjoy using data; you feel comfortable enough to try some new data approaches	You start to use data in basic ways at first, and forget that you "can't do it"; you are going along fine, and may get tripped up by a data glitch...but you are able to recover and learn from it	You participate in data-related meetings, You start to dig a little deeper into data review or tasks, and begin to ask more questions;	Continue to build and reinforce skills and confidence, and trust in your emerging skills versus regression to an earlier stage	Utilize your trusted data mentor or data coach to help you tackle more complex data issues; Keep using your data-fear Buster if you feel overwhelmed
Data Advocacy	COMFORT	You feel comfortable using data, and confident in your skills; you are excited about using data.	You begin to help others understand data and actively advocate for the use of data inside and outside of your organization	You understand the power of using and sharing data, and begin to help others use data and actively advocate for the use of data inside and outside of your organization	Maintain skills and enthusiasm; realize help from data mentors may sometimes be required	You have vanquished the fear monster – congratulations! Beware of imposter syndrome!

Source: Created by the authors.

Data Dread/Data Paralysis is the state at the "extreme fear" end of the data comfort continuum, where just considering the use of data terrifies you. It gives you the heebie-jeebies, and you may actually have a fight-or-flight reaction to being asked to do a data task...or you might just freeze, play dead like a possum, or curl up into a fetal position. Whatever the elements of the reaction, your reaction to the anxiety and fear you feel when confronted with a data task renders you unable to complete the task, further exacerbating your negative feelings toward data. The developmental tasks for these states are to, first, start to understand your fear and where it comes from, and second, start to consider that you may actually be able to change and move past the paralysis.

Data Dismissal/Data Avoidance is the fear state that flows from a significant fear of data.

Data Dismissal is the rejection of data and the importance of data and is based on extreme discomfort about your skills and abilities related to using data. By dismissing data as limiting or one-dimensional, or irrelevant to a particular endeavor, the individual minimizes the need to use data in their work. Data dismissal is often expressed with disdain, which may, in fact, serve as camouflage for a fear response: "If I reject the use of data, I won't have to use it."

Data Avoidance is the "passive" version of data dismissal, and may also serve to disguise fears regarding your data abilities. Instead of rejecting data and the importance of data, you avoid tackling data tasks, either directly, by saying you are too busy or using some other excuse, or indirectly, by "not picking up the data ball" when you have the opportunity. Either way, avoiding data means you are not using data that could potentially be very valuable, and you are not adding value to your organization in important ways.

The developmental tasks for these two states are learning some of the techniques to calm your feelings of anxiety, so you can rise above your fears enough to envision how data might actually be useful to the work.

Data Doubt to Data Acquiescence is the "transition" state on the data comfort continuum. In this state, data fear, avoidance, and dismissal can still be in play.

Data Doubt is characterized by a lack of trust in your own abilities, and also with what others may do with the data, but you realize that data are not going away, and you will likely have to engage with data.

Data Acquiescence is the point at which there is a shift, at least sometimes, to acquiescence-- thinking "ok...I'll take a look at the data." You accept that it is worthwhile to consider using data in your work, but you still find it challenging and intimidating.

The developmental tasks for data doubt and data acquiescence are beginning to utilize support and coaching to explore your newfound or newly discovered skills, and reinforcing your emerging ability to work with data.

Data Embrace is the state where you start to feel a level of comfort with data.

This is the point where you begin to regularly use data, sometimes in basic ways at first. You begin to participate in data related meetings, including asking questions and offering data-related answers.

As you begin to embrace date, "you are cooking with gas"; you begin to look forward to data tasks, and you find yourself actually volunteering for data tasks. There can also be a subsequent acknowledgment that data can provide valuable insight and that yes, collecting, analyzing, reporting, and even sharing data, often with the help of a trusted advisor, can be worth doing.

The developmental tasks for this state are building, reinforcing, and expanding your data-related skills and abilities.

Data Advocacy is the state in which you are regularly using data inside and outside of your organization.

Data Advocacy is the point at which, even when you are not sure you know how to do something, you try it; you get the technical assistance you need; you try different approaches; and finally, you feel empowered to take the next data steps. You may even begin to feel like you are a "data person."

This is the "actualized" state on the data comfort continuum. When you reach this state, you actually begin to help others to use data...not just in your organization, but also in your community. You point out opportunities to use data and try to ensure the use of data for important decisions. You definitely are considered a "data person" and maybe even a "data guru."

The developmental task for this stage is to maintain and trust your skills and enthusiasm; and beware of imposter syndrome!

Of course, even when you are actively advocating for the use of data and feel very comfortable with data, *fear and doubt can still creep in*…especially when interacting with other, more experienced data people, or when embarking on a new or unfamiliar data task, or using a new data tool. But when you feel these doubts, or experience imposter syndrome, that doesn't take you back to square one; movement along the data comfort continuum is both iterative and cumulative, and you should celebrate moving beyond those initial fear states whenever you are able.

The Role of Technology and Generational Issues

One thing experience has taught us is that change is hard for most of us; add in a dose of data fear, and it becomes harder. Advances in technology and being "chronologically gifted" can exacerbate the fear-change dynamic. We can get anchored in the technology we are used to, and when new technology comes around, it can be hard to keep up…and there is always a little fear that we won't be able to assimilate the new technology. Think of smartphone technology. Just the fact that there is a market for "simplified" phones for some folks is an example of this. You hear some older folks say, "I just want a simple phone, none of this other nonsense," but this is often because they are afraid to try to operate the newer phones, thinking that they may have serious difficulty understanding how to use them, and being intimidated by the fact that many new tools come without directions, or directions that are only offered online. When asked, many will admit that they would like to be able to send text messages, get onto social media sites, search the internet, or use the phone to count their steps, but the smartphone interface is so DIFFERENT from what they are used to that they balk. Saying they want to keep things simple is really a way of avoiding admitting they have trouble with the new interface, or haven't even tried because they are sure they will get confused and fail.

In a similar change dynamic, in 2020 the world as we knew it stopped. Around the world, people were required to refrain from in-person business, education, and socializing to try to stop the spread of the COVID-19 pandemic. This required most people to begin to use online meetings or educational technologies. There are multiple platforms, and some are easier to use than others, but all of them have required the user to adapt to a new, and more complicated way of connecting with colleagues, students, friends, and family members. This has been a challenge for all, and truly difficult for some people who are fearful of trying new technologies, and finding themselves overwhelmed by choices and directions they don't understand.

So it goes with data fear. Even when one has worked with numbers for a long time, it can be scary to move from a simple spreadsheet to a statistical program, or from issuing paper reports to posting interesting findings using a program like Tableau on the internet.

Notes

1 https://www.psychologytoday.com/us/basics/dunning-kruger-effect
2 Clance, P. R., & Imes, S. A. (1978). The imposter phenomenon in high achieving women: Dynamics and therapeutic intervention. *Psychotherapy: Theory, Research & Practice, 15*(3), 241–247. https://doi.org/10.1037/h0086006
3 See Grant, Adam, *Think Again* (2021), Viking: New York.

3

Fear Related to Capacity

Foundations of Fear: Fear of Math – "I can't do this"

A lot of people are afraid of math, or their ability to perform mathematical equations and understand concepts. They are afraid they can't understand the ideas, and/or believe they aren't smart enough to do math in the workplace – especially when it comes to understanding "data"; sometimes they don't understand presentations or papers by colleagues. That is intimidating. Also, many data tasks require the use of math directly, and as such, individuals who struggle with math fundamentals and fear math experience math anxiety when confronted with such data tasks. This can lead to many of the feelings and behaviors related to data fear that we described earlier in this book.

We are writing "they," but quite honestly, both Ron and Anne have experienced qualms about using math. For the first half of her career, Anne categorized herself as someone who was bad at math and was intimidated at the thought of having to "do math" at work.

Of course, fear of math is nothing new and has been at the core of discussions of poor standardized test scores at the elementary and high school level (and beyond) for a long time. There is even a term for an extreme version of it – mathemaphobia.[1] We do not have answers for preventing the development of these fears in the early years, although there are many promising approaches.[2,3] Nor do we contend that there are no

DOI: 10.4324/9781003496328-5

instances where an individual has cognitive processing or other learning disabilities that may contribute to genuine difficulties in understanding or undertaking math-related activities, thus contributing to the development of these fears. However, we do feel that in the vast majority of cases, these fears can be transcended.

There are lots of reasons why we develop our fears of math. They include bad teachers, lack of interest in the early days of educational careers, and failing to work at and/or grasp one or more key concepts upon which more work is based – thereby not understanding the concepts included in the next level.

In 1954, Sister Mary Fides Gough published an article in which she identified poor teaching as a major cause of what she termed "Mathemaphobia." Her article, "Why Failures in Mathematics? Mathemaphobia: Causes and Treatments"[4] describes a number of symptoms of "Mathemaphobia" and how they were either caused by lack of good teaching or could be "cured" by a good teacher spending the right amount of time and the right techniques with students.

We believe that in addition to the anxieties and deficits that some colleagues bring to the table, those of us who deal with data on a regular basis, and/or are comfortable in the data world, can add to the anxieties of our colleagues by our attitudes, our choice of language and terminology, and how we present mathematical/data-oriented concepts and ideas in the workplace. In effect, we are part of the problem.

Data Savvy People

There are many possible reasons why some colleagues or students are not comfortable with data. By creating an environment where they can become more comfortable understanding and using data, you can increase the capacity of your organization to utilize data to understand and improve performance. Create an environment where it is ok to make mistakes; learning is the goal, and not knowing something is an opportunity to learn, not a deficit.

When people begin to become more comfortable with data and start to feel their "data Wheaties," they can fall into the trap of using data jargon – arcane words that seem to proliferate in data circles. This use of jargon is unnecessary most of the time and serves to alienate those who may be less comfortable with data. Other associated behaviors are also alienating. When presenting data or speaking about data concepts, moving too fast...or, conversely, moving condescendingly slowly can make people less comfortable and data-anxious.

In ham-handed efforts to make things "sound easy," some of us tend to oversimplify concepts, which does not help people making initial forays into a world of data that can be pretty complex at times. This can be aggravated by speaking conceptually without using concrete examples or overestimating the universal applicability of a particular example. People struggling with data don't need these additional challenges.

Whatever the reason or reasons, people with math anxiety are not likely to engage in data-related work, and in our experience, they will go to significant lengths to avoid it.

For any organization, agency, or workplace to truly thrive, our math- and-data-averse colleagues need to be liberated from their fears and empowered to feel comfortable participating in data-related work. We have identified several ways that we, as colleagues, can facilitate that process (see Part IV).

Imposter Syndrome

As discussed earlier, imposter syndrome is a real condition that affects professionals in all fields and in all stages of their careers. Imposter syndrome[5,6] is the combination of thoughts, fears, and beliefs that you are not good enough, or not smart enough, or not experienced enough, or not learned enough for a position or role to which you have been invited, placed, or hired. It almost always includes the feature of worry that you will be discovered and exposed as, at best incompetent, and at worst, a fraud. There are many excellent resources on imposter syndrome, and we encourage you to consult them if you'd like to do some in-depth studying on the syndrome.

Imposter syndrome is insidious and, if not addressed, can become crippling.

We think the best way to address imposter syndrome is to acknowledge it and then move past it!! We realize that sounds cold; in fact, we believe the opposite is true! Let us explain:

We definitely understand, and have experienced, the feelings, thoughts, and self-judgment that are part of imposter syndrome: feeling like a fake; like you don't belong in a particular group or category of colleagues; like you are not qualified to be speaking at a conference, teaching a class, or listed as a subject matter expert – and, of course, the scariest one: being found out and exposed as a fake. Even when you are generally confident in your skills, and feel like you excel at your job, there can be situations where doubt creeps in. This can take you by surprise or be a recurring theme…but either way, it can prevent you from realizing your potential.

Once you understand imposter syndrome, and that most of us experience it at some time in our careers, it is important to assign it the appropriate level of unimportance. Yes, that is right: UNimportance. Early in this book, we wrote about the self-fulfilling prophecy of data fear. Imposter syndrome can work the same way: I think I can't; I think I can't; I think I can't…I can't.

An important first step is understanding that self-doubt is a very common experience, and that despite your insecurities, you can overcome it. Creating a list of your skills, your experience, and your qualifications is a powerful next step, and can become part of your fear-fighting toolbox, which we write more about in Part III of the book.

When you find yourself slipping into self-doubt, or wondering why you have been chosen to sit on a panel with a group of smart people – name imposter syndrome for what it is, take a deep breath, give yourself a moment of compassion, and then pull up your socks and move on. Go do your thing, and know that someone thought you were qualified enough to be where you are.

Conversely, you can indulge your feelings of insecurity and focus on why you are not good enough. This can lead to (either in the moment or subsequently) different manifestations of data fear, including data paralysis or fear of embarrassment that could actually affect how well you perform in the situation. This can become a crutch for not achieving your potential. It is our hope that since you are still reading the book this far in, you might believe that you can turn your data fear into data enthusiasm. Assigning imposter syndrome its appropriate level of UN importance is part of that process. We'll write more about this in Part III.

Notes

1   Gough, Sister Mary Fides, 1954. *The Clearing House*, Vol. 28, No. 5 (Jan., 1954), pp. 290–294 (5 pages), Published by: Taylor & Francis, Ltd.
2   Leinward, Stephen, 2014. *Principles To Actions: Ensuring Mathematical Success for All*. The National Council of Teachers for Mathematics.
3   Boaler, Jo, 2016. *Mathematical Mindsets: Unleashing Students' Potential through Creative Math, Inspiring Messages and Innovative Teaching*. Hoboken, NJ: Jossey-Bass.
4   Gough, Sister Mary Fides, 1954. *The Clearing House,* Vol. 28, No. 5 (Jan., 1954), pp. 290–294 (5 pages), Taylor & Francis, Ltd.
5   https://www.apa.org/gradpsych/2013/11/fraud.
6   Young, Valerie, 2011. *The Secret Thoughts of Successful Women: Why Capable People Suffer from Imposter Syndrome and How to Thrive in Spite of it*. New York: Random House.

4

Fear Related to Use

So far, we have been talking about fear of one's own capacity to work with data. But there is another whole category of fear, fear of data related to how that data will be used. These fears center on loss of control – control of the time spent on collecting data and reporting data, control related to what data gets reported and how it gets reported, and control related to how reported data are viewed, interpreted, and acted upon. Certainly, there can be real things to be afraid of here. There are instances where too much time is spent on data collection in relation to service provision, as well as instances when a lot of effort is put into collecting data that are never analyzed or utilized. There can be a substantial burden associated with compiling and reporting data, and if requests to do so are made in the face of an already large reporting burden, things can reach a saturation point. And, of course, once data are out in the world, you no longer control the information. There are also instances when data are misinterpreted and/or weaponized against those collecting and reporting the data. Sometimes data *do* reveal real performance deficiencies...which an organization may not be ready to tackle. While these things happen, and people are right to consider these risks, the ongoing need for data to drive decision-making and enhance transparency is great enough that overcoming the risks is necessary. Further, most of these potential risks also have strong potential benefits, like the ability to engage in data-informed decision-making, the opportunity to improve

DOI: 10.4324/9781003496328-6

performance based on what the data tell us, and even the opportunity to harvest a newly discovered trove of reports that are full of useful information. What is needed are effective strategies for dealing with fear related to these real concerns, and the skill and comfort to address mistakes, misinterpretations, and misuse. We offer these strategies in Part III of the book with our fear-fighting toolbox.

Data collection can be a huge burden, and many of us have experienced episodes where we thought that the time spent gathering and entering data has taken away from the time we could be spending with clients, or time actually doing whatever it was we were trying to accomplish. This can be exacerbated when funders or other stakeholders "stack on" more data collection requirements – sometimes requiring us to enter the same data into multiple systems. We can become legitimately concerned with this burden. However, we must balance this concern with an understanding that information about how we are delivering services, and the results of those services, will actually allow us to improve those services, demonstrate success, and sustain or grow funding levels in order to increase the amount of work we are able to deliver.

Many of us have also experienced desperately gathering and compiling data for reports, only to notice later that the reports just sit on the shelf and are never used. We may recognize the compliance nature of these reports, and even see some symbolic value in producing them, but when they are not used, it can definitely feel like they lack value, and that we have wasted a lot of time and energy in producing them. As we will see later, we need to do what we can to stop collecting data that are not really used and to build in ways of actually using the data we collect in meaningful attempts to understand processes, improve programs, and help clients achieve better outcomes.

When we honestly assess our data fears, we find they can be many and varied: fears related to how data will be used and misused; data collection and analysis feels like a waste of time because it takes focus away from service provision; the reports won't be used despite all the time we invest in creating them; the data will be used against us; the data will be misunderstood;

and perhaps the most scary – a combination of fears – lack of skill, combined with fear about use: if I don't get this reporting just right, they will use it to…(enter your own fear phrase here: punish our team; take away our funding….) and I won't be able to do anything to stop it. All of these fears are related to a loss of control regarding data and how it will be used.

In her article, "10 Reasons Why People Resist Change,"[1] Rosabeth Moss Kanter cites "loss of control" as the first reason why people resist change. She also cites uncertainty, loss of face, more work, and concerns about competence. As Kanter says, "change is resisted when people feel stupid." **So, the fears related to capacity we have discussed have a direct relationship to fears related to use.** When the need to perform new data tasks is encountered, these elements of resistance to change kick in. Many times over the course of our careers, we have experienced people resisting new data tasks, claiming other tasks are more important "it is more important to work with the client than it is to enter data" or that they are already doing too much "I just don't have time for this." This resistance could be grounded in inertia (the person resisting would simply rather continue to do things as they did before), or fear that they won't be able to do the tasks – arguing for not using or presenting data can be used as a device to hide fear of one's own capacity.

Uncertainty and loss of face could also come into play. Worries about collecting, analyzing, and releasing data may have to do with fear that data may be used as ammunition to reduce program budgets, downsize staff, or make other negative organizational changes: "They are going to use it against us!" As alluded to earlier, once data are out in the world, the promulgator of the data no longer controls the data – the essence of loss of control. Uncertainty as to how data will be interpreted or what reaction it will cause can instill fear. If there is a sense that the data will be perceived as deficient or reveal performance issues, there can also be fear of loss of face or embarrassment.

Paradoxically, we have found that acknowledging performance deficiencies and transparently discussing these issues and how they might be corrected, is a powerful way to deal with these fears. This can be a way to "reassert positive control," and stakeholders can react much more favorably to this approach than if you appear to be trying to sweep such performance issues under the rug, explain them away, or otherwise dodge responsibility for them.

When Anne was working in state government, she once had the opportunity to listen in as another agency explained why a promising program had performed poorly. Due to understaffing, the program was unable to achieve one of its primary outcomes: an outcome that would result in participants being better off AND lead to reimbursement for some program costs. The story and the factors identified helped the funders understand that in order to improve performance, the program in question truly needed increased staff resources to deliver services in a way that would ensure participants were better off after participation, and lead to the program being able to generate increased revenue in the future.

Similarly, we recently completed a report for a client that dealt with a challenging subject. We spent a significant amount of time exploring different aspects of the subject, and went to great lengths to delve into the information, utilizing both quantitative and qualitative data to provide the targeted information, context for the information, and potential solutions to the situation.

Our report was well-received, but one powerful person who read the report missed some of the important contextual information that explained why the situation existed, along with some very good recommendations for solutions from professionals in the field we were studying. This powerful person's reaction was to suggest eliminating an entire set of services and spending the saved money on something else. While we were horrified at the misinterpretation of the information, we were also confident enough in our skills, our work, and the information this person had missed, that we were able to stop the misinformed conversation, explain the importance of the underlying factors, and set up a time for a conversation to help the powerful person make a better-informed decision using the data that were actually presented, the story behind the data, and the proposed solutions.

Another way to reassert control is to provide a "story behind the data" you are reporting. Clearly explain any issues that you feel might be misinterpreted (without sounding like you are making excuses or trying to dodge responsibility), and discuss important dynamics that might explain changes or differences in performance levels, like differences in the composition of the clients your serve, environmental differences, or important events that might have had an impact on performance. We will discuss specific approaches to doing this in Part III.

Aside from what data might reveal about you, and how those data may be interpreted, working with data can include risks, especially considering legal issues related to data security and privacy. There may be legal issues related to accessing and/or sharing certain kinds of data (like classified data[2]), and you may be afraid that you could unknowingly violate the law. It is also true that you can unknowingly violate privacy provisions of certain laws, like FERPA[3] and HIPAA.[4] While these are very real concerns, with appropriate research, advice, and safeguards they are very manageable risks and are not by themselves a reason to not engage with, report, and use data.

Notes

1 https://hbr.org/2012/09/ten-reasons-people-resist-chang.
2 See United States Government Classification System, Executive Order 13526. https://en.wikisource.org/wiki/Executive_Order_13526.
3 The Family Educational Rights and Privacy Act. See https://www2.ed.gov/policy/gen/guid/fpco/ferpa/index.html.
4 Health Insurance Portability and Accountability Act. See https://www.hhs.gov/hipaa/for-professionals/index.html.

Part II

Assessing Our Abilities and Anxieties About Data

5

A Fear Self-Assessment

We have discussed the genesis and roots of data fear, the two major categories of data fear, and how data fear manifests itself within these categories. Often, people who fear data don't think about how and why they fear data, and how that impacts them and their work. We have developed a data fear self-assessment that can help identify in what ways data fear might be affecting you or those you work with. This can be the beginning of a more thorough examination of the data fear landscape for you, your work team, your organization, or others with whom you are working.

We have used this self-assessment in many training sessions and presentations on data fear and have collected the responses and analyzed them over time. We have used the results to refine the questions, and conducted a factor analysis (a statistical method to identify questions that move together in a similar fashion, suggesting that they measure different dimensions of the same concept, or factor) and reliability analysis (a statistical test that helps determine whether questions intended to measure a concept hold together as an index) to ensure the mix of questions work well together.

There are five primary components of the self-assessment:

♦ Imposter Syndrome Component
♦ Math and Developing Data Component
♦ Using Data Component

DOI: 10.4324/9781003496328-8

♦ Sharing/Reporting Data Component, Part 1 and
♦ Sharing/Reporting Data Component, Part 2

For each of the components, the self-assessment asks for the respondent's level of agreement with each statement regarding the respondent's self-perception and/or behavior.

Of course, this is a self-assessment, so it is important that the user be honest with themselves. It isn't a test, nor should it be seen as an opportunity to demonstrate mastery or acumen. The self-assessment is an opportunity for insight, and this opportunity is lost if answers are inflated (in either direction). Bottom line: there are no right or wrong answers; this is an opportunity for you to understand how data fear may be impacting your work, and will give you an opportunity to understand how to start addressing data fears or discomfort that get in your way.

The self-assessment tool itself (see appendix A) allows the user to first compare their level of agreement with each statement, total each rating for each component, and then also total the scores across components. The user can then look to see how they score for each component using the self-assessment score evaluator:

Interpreting Your Scores on the Fear Self-Assessment

Each of the five components has five questions, rated on a scale of 1–5, with a score of 1 representing very uncomfortable and 5 representing very comfortable.

Each component has a minimum score of 5 and a maximum score of 25.

The total score across all five components can range from 25 (totally uncomfortable) to 125 (extremely comfortable).

Interpreting Scores

See Table 5.1.

TABLE 5.1 Interpreting Self-assessment Scores

Score	Scoring For Each Subsection
25	Very Comfortable
20–24	Comfortable
15–19	Moderately Comfortable
10–14	Uncomfortable
5–9	Very Uncomfortable
Score	Overall Score
101–125	Very Comfortable
76–100	Comfortable
51–75	Moderately Comfortable
36–50	Uncomfortable
25–35	Very Uncomfortable

Source: Created by the authors.

Interpreting Scores and Understanding Variation in Your Answers

Questions within each component are intentionally similar, so scores within each component are likely to be consistent. Since questions in each component are about similar data-related issues, it is possible – but somewhat unlikely – for multiple questions to vary from the average response in each component. However, it is possible that the points for one of your answers in a section may vary from the rest of the answers in that section.

Variation in Scores within One of the Components

If one of your answers varies substantially from the others in the section, pay attention! This variation has the potential to be both informative and useful!

In components where you rated yourself as comfortable or very comfortable, an out-of-line response may illuminate a sub-topic that is less comfortable for you, indicating an area where you may want to focus your attention to increase your comfort or skill level. That might mean that while you are generally uncomfortable at the thought of creating data displays, you are comfortable when you are working in Excel and creating simple charts using the chart wizard.

In components where you rated yourself as uncomfortable or very uncomfortable, an out-of-line response will most likely identify a sub-topic where you feel more comfortable or more skilled. This indicates a potential area of strength, and will give you something on which to build as you continue to overcome your data fears.

In components where you rated yourself as somewhat comfortable, out-of-line responses could indicate either areas of strength or areas of greater discomfort.

Variation in Scores between the Five Components

Variations in scores between the three components can also provide useful information.

If your scores for one of the five components of the assessment are out of line with the others, that will give you the opportunity to understand, in a more general way, where your strengths and comfort lie, and where you are less comfortable. Use your areas of strength or greater comfort as a resource on which you can build your comfort in related areas.

The next section of the book includes descriptions of, and recommendations for using and creating your own, anxiety buster. Anxiety busters are relaxation and empowerment tools that we have created for ourselves over the years to combat our own fears about using data. For those of you who are totally overwhelmed by the thought of using data, we recommend spending the time to create your own anxiety buster, and get comfortable with feeling comfortable before moving on to the rest of the exercises in the section.

Part III

Addressing and Overcoming Data Fear: Taming the Fear Monster

6

A Fear-Fighting Toolbox

So far, we have been all about fear; but now, we are going to focus on what we can all do to vanquish the data fear monster. In developing the approaches that follow, we have drawn on our own personal experiences, our experiences as public sector employees and consultants, and a wide array of literature on dealing with fear and anxiety (Figure 6.1).

The fear-fighting toolbox contains an array of strategies and tools intended to help individuals transcend their data fears and increase their data comfort. We start with some general thoughts and stories that we think are helpful in getting into a "data engagement" mindset. We describe what we call a "data comfort learning model" that explains the basic way that we think about the data fear interventions we offer. We then discuss a particularly important foundational component – mindfulness – that we use in many of the subsequent tools we describe.

As you read through some of the strategies in our fear-fighting toolbox, you may notice that some of the tools and strategies we present are not specific to overcoming data fear and can be used in multiple types of situations. That is correct! The fact that they are generalizable does not make them less effective in fighting data fear; so, once you have learned to use them, and to make them "yours," consider utilizing them in other situations that cause you angst.

DOI: 10.4324/9781003496328-10

FIGURE 6.1 Toolbox fear monster.
Source: Liz Lahner drawnbyeal.com.

At this point, we move into the concrete tools that we believe will be very helpful. The first tools we describe are "Anne's Anxiety Buster" and "Ron's Anxiety Buster." We ultimately demonstrate how someone can build their own anxiety buster. We then talk about how the concept of "enlightened ignorance" can help to quell data fear and be used as a positive, value-added technique as one proceeds on their data-comfort journey. We also discuss recognizing what you don't know you know…and how positively identifying things you know can help you gain confidence. We offer some specific advice on mitigating risks associated with reporting and sharing data and promulgating data visualizations and data dashboards. Finally, we discuss how analysis doesn't have to be scary and how thinking about analysis using concrete, basic steps can help to minimize data fear.

New Data Practitioners

There is nothing to be ashamed of, or afraid of, related to starting your data journey from a place of fear. You can actually benefit from starting at a place of fear and transcending that fear, because once you have overcome the fear, you will end up comprehending the data fears that someone else experiences and that allows you to relate to and help others who suffer from data fear as they begin their journey

---

This Stuff Really Can Be Fun

ANNE: Recently, Ron and I were meeting about a project with a colleague of ours. The conversation turned toward some complex data collection and reporting issues that one of our clients needed to address. It was one of those tangled-up, chicken-or-egg situations, and the conversation followed the twists and turns of the situation. It was a little dizzying for me.

Ron and our colleague started talking about how much fun it would be to write a guidance document for our client that defined and explained the data challenges, outlined why they are important, and then offered a step-by-step data collection and reporting system that spanned multiple systems, and different types of services, and the types of analyses that would need to be performed.

They then, jokingly, asked me if I would like to take the first stab at writing it up. All I could think was: FUN?? How could this be fun? This is way too intimidating to be fun!

Then, I realized that whether this project was intimidating, or whether it was fun, was up to me AND HOW I PERCEIVED IT! And I have choices about how I perceive working with data.

I can freak out, like I would have done in the past when I didn't believe I could be a data person. I can also use some of the approaches we talk about in this book, and look at this as a puzzle to be solved. The first thing I need to remember is to chill out, and take some deep breaths to get some oxygen to my brain, so I can get centered and create my roadmap to success!

RON: Some may hear my pronouncements about data work being "fun" and immediately think: "weirdo," or "geek." And while they may be right on both counts, I feel the need to defend my statement. "Deconstruction is a core analytic concept that we will reference several times in this book." Let's deconstruct "fun." What makes something fun? First, I think, fun is the opposite of boring. When doing something fun our brain lights up. We are *engaged*. We are **interested**. At least sometimes, this engagement and interest comes from something that *challenges* us. Not in a threatening, "struggle to survive" kind of way, but in a safe, "let's see if I can do this, see if I can prevail" kind of way. This can be fun even if your skill set is not fully developed. I played basketball all through my teenage years. I was never very good at it, but I did get better at it over the years, and playing challenged me, and it was FUN.

ANNE: ok – so first step is to chill out and apply either Anne's anxiety buster or Ron's anxiety buster, and realize there is a whole new way to think about this kind of stuff……..maybe I can think of it as a game…

RON: Now let's apply this to data work. Even if your skills are not fully developed, isn't it better to look upon a data task as an adventure? Something that's engaging? Something, dare I say it, that can be fun? First, I will admit that not ALL data work is fun. Sometimes you have to do stuff (like do data entry, or clean up data that has a lot of errors in, or produce the same report for the 20th time) that is not fun. But lots of data tasks, and data challenges are fun. Here are some of my favorite "data puzzles" and challenges:

  ◆ Figuring out what outcome(s) a program is intended to produce
  ◆ Identifying how to measure the achievement of those outcomes

- Developing survey questions, especially questions that can be used together to indirectly measure a concept that can't be measured directly
- Developing the best data display for the data that I want to discuss
- Coming up with a "data story," including sequencing the presentation of data
- Identifying relationships between different kinds of data in a performance report
- Looking at trend data to see if there is something interesting going on in the trend
- Looking at performance data and going through a "diagnostic" process to determine possible causes of poor performance
- Weaving qualitative and quantitative data into the fabric of an analysis

All of these things can be challenging, sometimes requiring considerable effort. But they can all be fun – if you let them be.

ANNE: Honestly Ron – when I first read your list, I didn't necessarily think most of the items looked very fun, but when I read through them again, I realized that most of what you listed isn't number-crunching. It is really more like detective work, and understanding stories, or helping people to figure out what the stories are. I think it is safe to say that they all start out with asking yourself "Hey – what is going on here, and how do we either understand it, or help someone else understand it?"

I almost got a little anxious when I read the last one: "weaving qualitative and quantitative data into the fabric of an analysis." Then, I realized I needed to practice what I am preaching, and I took a big breath and asked myself what you meant with those words. When I remembered this was supposed to be fun, I realized you were just talking about using both numbers and stories to create a story that is both interesting and helps people to understand what the data are telling us – right?

Over the next few pages, we will be transitioning into some specific tools you can use to start feeling more comfortable with data, starting with objectively thinking about your data fear, and then creating your own steps to addressing, and ultimately overcoming, your own data fear.

First, we describe our approach to overcoming data fear: The Data Comfort Learning Model.

The Data Comfort Learning Model

Progress along the data comfort continuum that we described on page 29 typically will not "just happen," especially if you are experiencing intense data dread or data paralysis. Progress usually requires effort and the application of some basic tools. We call our learning model the "managed fear" model. As you can see from the figure below, when fear is not managed, it creates a negative feedback loop. You begin with fear: fear emotions lead you to behave in certain negative ways, for which there can be negative consequences, which tend to only reinforce the negative starting condition (Figure 6.2).

In the unmanaged fear model, your starting condition is one of fear. That fear manifests itself in a range of emotions that can span anxiety, panic, dread, and doubt. The consequence of not managing those fears is the creation of a set of behaviors that are correlated to these emotions. They include paralysis, dismissal, and avoidance. By not managing your fears, you actually reinforce them, and you find yourself stuck in the belief that

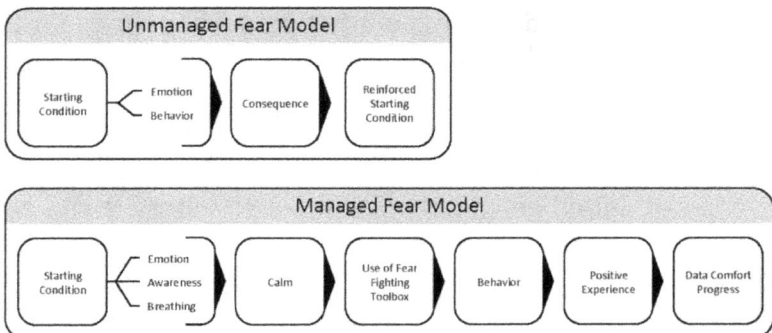

FIGURE 6.2 Unmanaged and managed fear models.
Source: Created by the authors.

your data fear is warranted, and you are doomed to be a failure at working with data.

In a managed fear approach, you may begin with negative emotions, but you have strategies to manage them, so instead of reinforcing your feelings of fear, you are able to intervene in the fear process by acknowledging your feelings and utilizing some breathing exercises so that you calm down, use specific tools that we share in the fear-fighting toolbox, and modify your behavior, which results in better outcomes, thus reducing fear and resulting in progress on the data comfort continuum. This is the basic process within which the fear-fighting tools are used. Acknowledging the fear and breathing make up the first step on the journey to being comfortable working with data.

The First Step on a Data-Comfort Journey

We define data comfort as **feeling at ease enough to effectively engage with data, in order to use data to understand the world, solve problems, and make a difference in organizations.** This level of comfort is important in order to overcome the fear that can inhibit us from effectively engaging with data and not allowing data fear to create a barrier to using data.

The first step on the journey toward data comfort is acknowledging your fear and sitting with that acknowledgment, while making sure you breathe slowly and deeply to keep the oxygen flowing to your brain.

As one resource suggests, deep breathing is one of the best ways to lower stress in the body. This is because when you breathe deeply, it sends a message to your brain to calm down and relax. The brain then sends this message to your body. Those things that happen when you are stressed, such as increased heart rate, fast breathing, and high blood pressure, all decrease as you breathe deeply to relax.[1]

Next, we will walk you through some steps that help you to consider thinking about data in a different way. Understand that you may still feel anxious thinking about data and being aware of that can open your mind to starting to feel comfortable with data.

The strategies we share in this section start with taking small, tentative, first steps toward data comfort. They allow you to celebrate little victories overcoming your fear. We then introduce you to a more robust discussion of relaxation and mindfulness, followed by the anxiety-busting exercises that we developed to empower ourselves. Finally, we guide you through developing your own anxiety buster so that you can tame your data fear monster.

Data Meditation: Getting Started on the Journey

Let's begin the journey by thinking about what life would be like if you weren't afraid of engaging with data. We realize even thinking about engaging with data can be anxiety-provoking; so, let's start with some deep breathing and visioning:

- ◆ Start by making yourself comfortable; relax by practicing some deep-breathing exercises. If you aren't sure how to practice deep-breathing exercises, there are lots of great websites that can help you feel comfortable with deep breathing. Here are a couple we like:

   https://healthy.kaiserpermanente.org/health-wellness/health-encyclopedia/he.stress-management-breathing-exercises-for-relaxation.uz2255

   healthline.com/health/breathing-exercises-for-anxiety

- ◆ While you continue to breathe deeply and feel relaxed, consider the possibility that there might be a place in your work for data *if you could move past your fear*

- ◆ Continue breathing deeply to stay relaxed, and visualize a conversation with a data-savvy friend or colleague. How would they answer the following questions?
  - ◆ Why does data matter?
  - ◆ What can I learn from data?
  - ◆ Why do I need to understand data?
  - ◆ What can data help me understand
  - ◆ Why do I need to use data?

♦ How can data help me understand things better?
♦ How can using data help me be more effective?

As a next step, review these questions again. Visualize the answer you would give as if you were the data-savvy colleague. Can you see the possibility that if you didn't fear working with data, you might be able to see the possibility of using data? Imagine what it is like to be instilled with confidence and invested in data power!

Data Meditation: What Your Eyes See

Many people with high levels of data fear have a visceral reaction to seeing a chart – even a simple chart – either rapidly pushing the offending document with the chart in it aside, or simply "reading around the chart" and avoiding actively engaging with it. Either of these approaches can result in accepting others' interpretation as factual without testing it against the figure, or without determining what other insights can be gained from the information available.

Public policy and administration professor Meg Streams (Tennessee State University) developed the following exercise:[2]

Looking at the following data display, what are **two (2) distinct one-sentence factual claims that one could appropriately justify using this figure** (there are more than two possible!) Your claims must be both deducible from, and consistent with, the information in the figure (Figure 6.3).

Think about your two statements before continuing to read this meditation!

When looking at any chart, consider questions like these:

♦ There are three different groups represented in the data …what are they?
♦ There are three different data series shown on the chart… which one is associated with which group? Does each data series represent a distinct sub-group or is one a combination of the others?

Percentage of Students Chronically Absent

	2017-18	2018-19	2019-20	2020-21	2021-22
--- Overall	25.3%	25.4%	27.9%	44.0%	46.0%
—— Eligible for Free Lunch	28.8%	28.9%	31.3%	50.2%	51.3%
– – Not Eligible for Free Lunch	11.7%	12.4%	12.3%	11.7%	25.6%

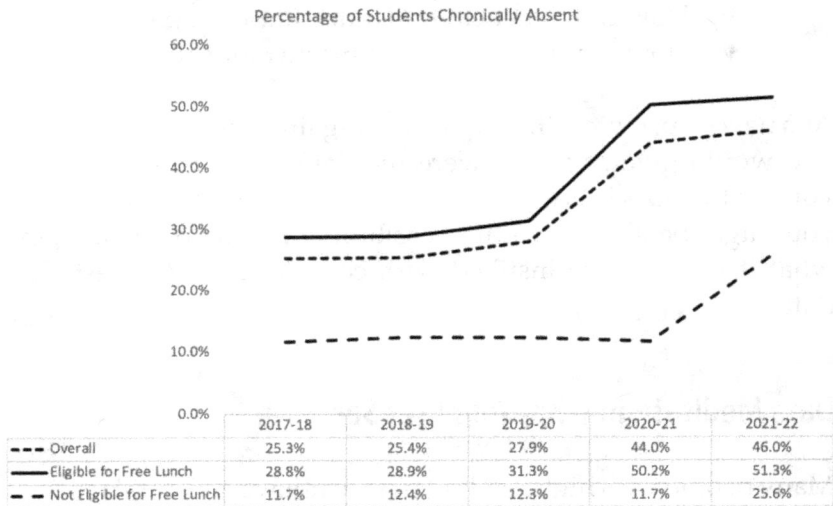

FIGURE 6.3 Chronic absenteeism.
Source: Created by the authors.

◆ What is the relationship between the data for each group?
◆ What do the marks represent; am I seeing the mark of individual data points, or a line, curve, or area constructed from those marks, or both? (In this example, the data points are not marked, only connected, and the reader needs to recognize that there is one data point per school year.)

Some of the statements that could be made include:

◆ The overall annual rate of chronic absenteeism in Hartford Public Schools has increased beginning in the 2020–2021 school year
◆ The annual rate of chronic absenteeism among Hartford School Districts eligible for free lunch increased beginning in 2020–2021 – the first full school year of the COVID-19 pandemic – while the rate among those not eligible did not increase until 2021–2022
◆ The rate of chronic absenteeism for those eligible for free lunch is substantially higher than the rates for those not eligible across the five school years shown

◆ The rate of chronic absenteeism for those eligible for free lunch is higher than the overall rate of chronic absenteeism in Hartford School District for the five school years shown

◆ The largest gap in chronic absenteeism rates between HSD students eligible for free lunch and those not eligible over the five school years examined occurred in 2020–2021

◆ Since these data represent annual observations, we cannot tell whether absenteeism among any group of Hartford students began to rise following the pandemic onset in Spring 2020, or not until the 2020–2021 school year had begun [this is a statement that is factual about what we *can't* tell rather than what we can – but also an important kind of realization to have.]

These statements can be made with little or no subject matter knowledge, just by carefully scrutinizing the data. This starts with looking at the elements that make up the chart. What does the Y (vertical) axis represent (in this case, the percentage of students chronically absent)? What does the X (horizontal) axis represent (in this case, the different school years presented on the chart)?

Approach any data display with fresh eyes, whether or not you know the core subject matter; deconstruct the data display and ask these kinds of questions (the exact questions will vary based on the kind of data display you are looking at), and you will find the data displays will yield to your analytic prowess and interpretative skill.

Data Mindfulness

Jon Cabot Zinn defines mindfulness as "the awareness that arises from paying attention, on purpose, in the present moment and non-judgmentally."[3] Paying attention, being aware of what is happening and what you are thinking and feeling in the moment, is a very important tool. Throughout the remainder of the book, we will note how mindfulness can help you to recognize when you are in a "fear state," identify what you are feeling, and begin to unpack those fears. We call this "data mindfulness."

Data mindfulness can help you better understand your relationship to data, and the place of "you and the data" in the universe. It is one thing when you are working with data in order to decide, for example, a relatively minor thing like who to assign the next case to, and another thing when you are working with data to defend your organization from a budget cut, and still yet another if you are using data to decide what to do in an emergency or crisis situation. Being mindful of what anxieties and fears those different situations might propagate in you can be very enlightening, and can be very useful in empowering you to understand your fear response, and take the right action to address the fear and move forward in the work.

Data mindfulness can help you find meaning in your analytic activities and in the data themselves. Why are you looking at data in the first place? Rather than performing some calculations (or performing an elaborate analysis, or building a data visualization) in a rote manner (mechanically checking it off the list, like "ok, that's DONE"), be more aware of the value and the reasons why you are engaging with the data. "This could crack the whole thing open!" "This could save us so much time!" "If I do this right, this could really strengthen our grant proposal!" "If I display these data correctly, I could really make a strong case for that new approach!" This helps to build a relationship between you and the data. You will find such relationships are symbiotic...the more you engage with data, the more you will find value in doing so, and the more the data will speak to you, prompting you to ask more questions and engage with the data further.

Here are the ways that both of us started to become comfortable with using data. Anne's Anxiety Buster is mostly related to her fear of lack of capacity; Ron's Anxiety Buster is mostly related to fear of how the data could be used.

Anne's Anxiety Buster

When I was a college student, I didn't always study enough for exams or presentations. That caused me to be unprepared, and I experienced the dread and panic that is the result of not being ready for a test, or feeling that I didn't have command of my subject matter in a presentation.

I developed an approach to those situations that worked pretty well, and through the subsequent decades, I have modified that approach so that it works for me when I suffer from imposter syndrome, or when I am under a lot of pressure on a project, or when I have to give a presentation or teach something about which I don't feel qualified – you know.....those times when data feel like a four-letter word.

Before we jump into my anxiety buster, let me clarify that this isn't about pretending I know something I don't know. Rather, the anxiety buster is part of my fear-fighting toolbox. I use it when I doubt myself and what I know, and I need to gather my thoughts and remember how to use them. It is how I get centered and find my self-confidence.

Here are the steps to my anxiety buster – see how they work for you, and feel free to modify them and create your own anxiety buster!

1. Recognize the Fear
    The first step is realizing that I am starting to freak out, to doubt myself, to doubt my abilities, and to envision failure as the likely outcome - probably accompanied by embarrassment. When I recognize that I am feeling overwhelmed and data-anxious, I realize I can change the narrative playing in my head; I am empowered to take control.
2. Breathe
    After identifying the anxiety I am experiencing, I remember to breathe. Sending oxygen to my brain puts me in a better place to look at the situation objectively. I consider that the task may not be impossible. I realize I may not be destined to fail and be discovered as a fake. Success could actually be a possibility!

3. Center My Thoughts

For me, this used to mean a prayer to St. Jude, the patron saint of hopeless causes, asking for help in creating the presence of mind so that I could remember what I already knew. Use what works for you: get centered, or call on your higher power, or put it out to the universe. The idea is to get out of the flight-or-fight response by breathing and allowing ourselves to acknowledge that we actually do know something about the topic at hand, and the task is to retrieve that knowledge, instead of continuing to freak out.

4. Know Your Know

My grandmother used to say, "Everybody knows his own know." That idea is powerful here because it is important for me – and maybe you – to remember that I know what I know, and to be grounded by, and to focus on, that knowledge. I can use the knowledge I have to tackle the problem at hand. Instead of doubting my knowledge and experience, I can use my knowledge to help me understand and analyze the situation. It is part of my strength.

5. Review the Task

I go back to the data, problem, or situation itself. I look at it again with my newly empowered mindset. Now, I can be more objective about the information

◆ What is the actual task at hand?
◆ What does the written information tell me?
◆ What do I need to do with it?
◆ Is the information clear?
◆ Does it require some decoding?
◆ Can I break it down into smaller segments that are easier to understand or tackle?

6. Dissect the Problem

Once I feel more in control and have considered the task more objectively – while continuing to breathe so that my brain keeps working – I can break down the task, problem, or assignment into smaller tasks or questions that are easier to answer or analyze. (hmmm… this doesn't seem quite so impossible… success might really be a possibility.)

7. Reinforce my Ability to Handle the Situation

As I am starting to address the challenge in a more objective and reasonable way, I know that I might still struggle with the task. It is important for me to remember that the problem may not be my inability to understand something, or not being smart enough to figure it out; it just might be a flawed assignment, task, or piece of information I am encountering.

Realizing that I might be identifying a problem or mistake that someone else made is counter-intuitive to me. It is much easier for me to assume that the mistake or lack of understanding is on my part, not someone else's part, and I need to remember the possibility that the fault doesn't lie within my understanding of the situation. Sometimes I need to go through previous steps in this exercise one, or more, times to make sure I am not missing something. Going through those steps again has a couple of benefits: it reinforces the process; and it allows me to engage in some metacognition, or thinking about what I am thinking about, or in my grandmother's words: knowing my own know – and knowing that I know it!

Sometimes I find that I missed something in my first review and dissection, and that is ok because I have identified it on the second review. Other times, I realize that I have encountered something that was confusing, poorly constructed, or just plain wrong.

Either way, I am on my way to a solution.

8. Ask for Help If I Need It

If I understand, and feel prepared to handle the data challenge after going through the first seven steps in busting my anxiety, that is great, and I will proceed. However, if the problem is still vexing me, it may be time to ask for help as a reasonable option.

No one knows everything, and once I have gone through the steps of busting the anxiety so that I have been able to objectively consider the task, assignment, or data, I may need someone with a different skill set to help me work through it; and I may ask a trusted colleague to help me decode the problem.

I may need someone with more data experience to help me decode a document so that I can begin to participate in the conversation or task.

This is where I can put my enlightened ignorance to work (read more about enlightened ignorance a little later in this book). When I ask questions, I learn something new. I can use this situation as an opportunity to increase my knowledge.

I have busted my anxiety, by relaxing, breathing, "knowing my know," and maybe even asking for help. I move ahead, empowered to take on my task.

Ron's Anxiety Buster

Many people feel anxiety, discomfort, or agitation when they are considering sharing or reporting data, especially if the data are being reported for the first time, or if the data could be misinterpreted or misused. When I encounter these "data qualms," I don't ignore those signals. They may very well be warning signs that need to be attended. But I also do not allow myself to launch into what can be a very natural and intuitive reaction – that is, I don't leap to "we can't share that" or "there's going to be trouble if we report that," or, worse, simply "no way."

1. Acknowledge the Signals
   Instead, I try to *acknowledge* the signals my mind is sending. I say, ok…there is some perceived or real danger here that I need to think about.
2. Breathe
   I then *breathe*. I take a few moments to center myself, and try to get the rational part of my brain working again. Breathing helps to attenuate the visceral reactions I might otherwise be having, triggered by fear or anxiety.
3. Identify the Danger

Once I have stabilized myself a bit, I try to *identify* the danger…what IS it that I am afraid of? I may even do an informal *risk assessment* to try to fully understand what I am afraid might happen if the data are shared or reported: Depending on the circumstance, I might be afraid of one particular, specific danger, like "the Governor is going to HATE this." Other times, the danger may be less specific, like "people aren't going to understand why our performance declined," or "people are going to see this and jump to the wrong conclusions." Whether specific or generalized, there is usually some essential risk underlying our fear, such as:

◆ Misinterpretation of the data being reported
◆ Uncertainty as to what someone might do with the data
◆ Getting "blamed" for poor data quality or poor performance
◆ Having resources taken away due to poor performance
◆ Feeling "embarrassed" at poor performance

Whatever the essential risk, it is important to remember two things: (1) the risk is often real, and we cannot "wish" the risk away; and (2) there is almost always something you can do to manage and mitigate these risks.

4. Develop a Risk Management Approach

Once I have identified the risks I am afraid of, I develop a *risk management approach*. And, having gone through this process a few times, I often use the same general approaches can often be used when new data sharing or reporting qualms arise.

Below are some risk management strategies that can help for some of the risks mentioned above.

I find that once I identify appropriate risk management strategies, I feel a lot better about the data sharing or reporting I am considering.

5. Get Help If Needed

Of course, sometimes I'm not able to identify an appropriate risk mitigation strategy on my own. I find that

Risk	Risk Management Strategy
People are going to misinterpret the data	Never just report data; always include a "data story" that explains any hard-to-understand aspects of the data being reported, as well as sharing the context – what environmental or other factors may have contributed to the data being what it is
Getting "blamed" for poor data quality or poor performance, or simply feeling embarrassed by poor performance	Start with the first strategy, always including a data story and context. This gives you the opportunity to explain what is happening and avoids people jumping to conclusions. Add to that offering possible solutions…those that you may have already embarked on as well as those you could try. If you have tried something that hasn't worked, say that too; it shows you are actively seeking a solution, and precludes someone from saying, "why didn't you just try X?"
Using poor performance as a reason to take resources away from you	Use the first two strategies. Also, include a balanced array for measures in your report; do not report one measure in isolation, even an important outcome measure, because it often doesn't provide a comprehensive picture of what is happening. Reporting multiple measures also may help you establish that a program is being well run…and still experiencing lower-than-expected outcomes, or help you show that some other dynamic, like a change in the mix of customers served, that does not necessarily have to do with the core value of the program
Uncertainty as to what people will do with the data	While it is always possible that somebody might do something radical with the data, the other risk management strategies mentioned here will probably mitigate risks related to most unforeseen uses of the data

"getting a little help from your friends" can do the trick. Sometimes it is just a question of talking through the risk with someone who has experience with a similar circumstance or issue. Sometimes, in order to implement a specific risk management approach, I may need to surmount other technical issues. Here, I might run into fears related to my capacity associated with those technical issues. Asking friends for help – and by extension, getting additional technical assistance or training…is important here.

6. Be Honest with Yourself

This leads to another aspect of all of this...that sometimes, maybe, the fear that you might actually VOICE is NOT really the fear that you are actually EXPERIENCING. Humans being human, it may sometimes be easier to voice a fear related to USING data rather than acknowledging a fear of your own lack of capacity. Be mindful of this, back at the fear acknowledgment stage, and be honest with yourself about what you are really afraid of, and act accordingly (see Anne's Anxiety Buster, for starters).

I have found that following the above steps puts me in a place where my fears are attenuated, and I feel better prepared to tackle the task at hand.

Creating Your Own Anxiety Buster

You have read how we overcome our anxiety related to data; in this section, we list the basic components of both sets of anxiety busters so that you can create your own anxiety buster. We encourage you to spend some time thinking about the following steps, and how you can personalize them to create your own empowerment process for dealing with your data fear.

Pull out a sheet of paper, or start a new document on your screen, and map out your own anxiety buster by going through the following steps. Don't expect that you will identify all the steps to your anxiety buster the first time you try; this is likely to be an iterative process and will become more useful the more you think about it, and the more you practice.

Step 1: Recognize the fear

Both Ron and Anne recognize the signals that tell them they are getting close to the data fear monster's lair. For Ron, it includes sweaty palms and trouble focusing on other tasks. For Anne, it includes a general feeling of anxiety and a sudden need to clean out junk drawers and closets – anything to avoid the task at hand. The important thing is to be able to identify the warning signals that you could be headed for a meltdown.

◆ Take some time to see if you can identify some or all of your fear signals, and write them down

Step 2: Breathe to get re-centered

This step is pretty universal. It is also pretty important. For Ron, breathing helps him to get re-centered and to start thinking rationally. For Anne, taking some deep breaths gets her out of a fight-or-flight mentality and allows her to start thinking more positively.

◆ Spend a couple of minutes taking some long, deep breaths and see if you feel a little more centered

◆ Go all out and actually smile (go on – no one is watching) and feel the difference throughout your body[4]

The point of step 2 is to start to relax and reframe the situation from an anxiety, or fear frame, and into one where you allow yourself to think and feel in a more hopeful frame of mind

Step 3: Diagnose the fear-generating issue, and what you are afraid of (what is this anxiety all about?)

Ron works to identify the danger and tries to figure out what he is afraid of. He might even do an informal risk assessment to play out what he is afraid might happen. He has found it is important to be honest with himself – sometimes the fear that he first identifies is not really the underlying fear: Ron explains that it can be easier to voice a fear about how someone else might use the data rather than admitting to oneself that it is ones' own lack of capacity that is causing the fear.

For Anne, this step includes getting centered and opening herself up for help. (Anne says a quick prayer for help; for others, this could include calling on your higher power, putting it out to the universe, or just continuing to breathe deeply.) Once centered, she will go through a series of questions about the specific fear-generating issue at hand.

◆ Here are some questions to ask yourself that may be useful as you identify the issues related to your task.

Feel free to add or change questions so that this step is useful for you:

♦   What is the real problem?

♦   Is it how data will be used, or your capacity to use data?

♦   If it is your capacity, what are you afraid of?

♦   Can you identify the root cause or source(s) of these fears?

♦   If it is about how data will be used, what are you afraid of?

♦   Are you worried the data could be weaponized against you?

♦   Are you concerned that you won't be able to explain the data; or be able to overcome someone else's misinterpretation of the data?

♦   What else might be making you anxious related to this data task?

♦   List everything – even if it feels trivial or silly

Once you understand what is going on for you, you can begin to address the anxiety.

Create your own steps to bust your anxiety:

Step 4: Think about solutions that work for you:

This is an opportunity to tap into some of your effective coping strategies – these can be strengths you take for granted, or may not even realize you have. They are solutions and strategies that you may use in other areas of your life. Take some time and reflect back on how you handle stressful or anxiety-producing situations.

♦   What relaxes you and/or calms you down? Possibilities could include taking a walk, exercising, listening to music, talking to a friend, spending time with a pet

♦   What centers you? This might be the same as what relaxes you, or it might be something more intentional like meditating, reviewing your accomplishments, organizing your desk, "knowing your know" or something else that helps you gather your wits, and get ready to move forward

◆ What are your strengths that you bring to this situation? We tend to forget our positive qualities and strengths when we are caught in the throes of the data fear monster. What are some of the strengths that have allowed you to succeed in other areas of your life? That might include having a logical mind, being detail-oriented, being able to see "the big picture," managing a project, or overseeing a client's progress on a case.

◆ How can you use some or all of those strengths in this instance?

Step 5: Review the task and identify the method you will use in order to overcome this anxiety

You have identified that you are experiencing a fear or anxiety reaction, done some deep breathing, and maybe even smiled at yourself, diagnosed what the fear is about, relaxed and centered yourself, and remembered your strengths. You are ready to bust your anxiety!

When we get to this point, Anne asks herself a series of questions to help break down the task into manageable pieces that she can start to tackle. Ron performs an informal risk analysis and develops a risk management approach.

◆ Consider the strengths that you have identified for yourself, and the strategies that work for you in other kinds of situations, and how they can help you in this situation

◆ Go back to the data, problem, or situation itself, and look at it again with your newly empowered mindset. Be more objective about the information and your ability to handle it.

Step 6: Create your action steps to successfully navigate through the situation:

For Anne, this means reviewing the task and dissecting it into small chunks she can handle

For Ron, this means creating a risk management strategy

◆ Keeping your strengths and successful strategies in mind, realize that you can handle this situation

- ◆ Identify which of your strengths and strategies will help you bust your anxiety and address the issue at hand
- ◆ Decide what you are going to do to solve the issue – or to at least relieve your anxiety so that you can work on solving the issue from a strength-based frame
- ◆ Write down the strengths and strategies you will employ – you may find that you come to regularly rely on a group of strengths and strategies that become your go-to tools for busting your anxiety

Step 7: Ask for help if you need it

It Might Not Be You!

Those of us who doubt our data skills usually assume that if we don't understand a data chart or display, or how a set of numbers add up, it is due to our lack of skill or comprehension. The truth is that everyone makes mistakes sometimes, and if you are looking at the data carefully, you might perceive a mistake in the numbers. Due to your doubt about your own skills, you may be hesitant to question the numbers. An approach that has worked for us is asking for help in understanding the numbers. That gives the creator of the data chart an opportunity to explain what you are not understanding or the opportunity to correct a mistake they have made. When it is the latter, most people will congratulate you on finding the error, and thank you for helping them correct it. Additionally, not all data displays are created equal, and people are not equally skilled at creating great data displays; so, any particular data display you are presented with may include mistakes – you should not jump to the conclusion that you are missing something or not capable of understanding the meaning or the implications of the data display – it may, in fact, just be poorly executed. If that is true, this is another opportunity to ask for help in understanding the display and maybe even make some gentle suggestions for improvement of the data display.

We all struggle sometimes, and asking for help from a trusted colleague or mentor can help you get through a situation that you can't solve alone, and it is also an opportunity to learn new anxiety-busting steps from a trusted support person.

Anne has a small group of trusted colleagues she knows she can go to for some assistance when she needs some help solving a problem or decoding some data. For Ron, sometimes it is just a question of talking through the risk with someone who has experience with a similar circumstance or issue. Sometimes, in order to implement a specific risk management approach, he may need to deal with other technical issues, and he realizes he might experience fears related to his capacity associated with those technical issues.

The Gift That Doesn't Feel Like a Gift: When Data Fear Can Inspire or Motivate Us

We give much attention in this book to acknowledging and understanding how fear can inhibit and block us from working with data. There are some instances, however, when a low level of anxiety and dissatisfaction with our usual way of dealing with data can inspire and motivate us in our data work, or guide us to the appropriate level of coaching or instruction to get past the fear and empower us to begin the work. In effect, the negative situation becomes a "gift" in that it motivates us to change and grow. There are two instances, in particular, where this can be true in the context of this book: when you recognize that it is just a lack of training that stands in the way of you being able to perform an important or desirable function; and when you are able to understand and embrace your enlightened ignorance, which we will discuss later, as a way to begin to formulate questions and ideas that help you view data as potentially approachable. Before we start exploring these two dynamics, it is important to acknowledge two additional factors related to the gift:

1. The "gift" NEVER feels like a gift when you are in the middle of receiving it. It takes a little reflection and distance to realize that what feels like a threat is actually an opportunity IF you treat it as one
2. If you are in the throes of data dread or data paralysis, you may not yet be in a place to benefit from these "gifts." Don't worry – growth comes in steps and stages; as you move through the data comfort continuum, you may find that you are ready to consider lack of training and enlightened ignorance, gifts from which you can potentially benefit.

Anne once had a supervisor who consistently expected her to perform data-related tasks that were outside of her job responsibilities. They were also outside of her skill set and therefore way outside of her comfort zone. It was incredibly frustrating and intimidating until Anne realized that instead of sitting with her fear, she would benefit from learning the required skills. They weren't part of her job, but learning the skills would allow her to grow professionally and could also help with overcoming her fears of using data. She overcame the fear enough to learn the skills and, in doing so, found that she enjoyed and understood the work well enough that she was in a position to start helping other colleagues to overcome their fears and learn the same skills.

Dealing with the demands from an unfair supervisor was not enjoyable, but by realizing that she could turn the situation into a positive experience for herself and others, Anne overcame those fears, empowered herself by learning new skills, and lived happily ever after...except for that pesky boss ☺.

Embracing your Enlightened Ignorance

There are plenty of things that each one of us doesn't know. Socrates claimed that the only true wisdom is in knowing you know nothing. And honestly – it is fair to say that for most of us, we don't know all of the things we don't know – because we don't know. Right?

Many people go through life comfortable knowing what they know, and not knowing what they don't know. But every once in a while – maybe when we are trying to understand what a data set is trying to tell us, or following a presentation that uses unfamiliar concepts or language – some of us realize that we are missing a piece of information, or we don't have some kind of knowledge that we need. This realization is called "Enlightened Ignorance." We describe it as realizing that there is "something I don't know, and that I want to know. There is some piece of knowledge that is out of my reach for now; and now that I realize it, I want to know it." McGill University Professor Emeritus, and Torah scholar, Yaakov Brawer describes this state as "Essential Ignorance" and describes it as "not a lack of awareness, but rather the awareness of a lack." Essential ignorance is achieved when a person becomes truthfully and sincerely cognizant that he lacks understanding. In contrast to passive ignorance, essential ignorance represents a relatively advanced state of self-comprehension.[5]

It is tempting to focus on the "lack" instead of the "awareness"; when we focus on the lack, specifically "our lack," that can move us right back into fear-based thinking (remember our diagram and explanation of fear-based thinking versus a managed-fear approach) and doubting our own competence. Many emerging data practitioners take a step backward at this point, and they lean into that fear-based thinking: I am not smart enough; I don't know enough; everyone in this meeting will think I am stupid because I don't know this.

Don't fall into that trap!

We can almost guarantee that there are other people sitting around the same table as you and silently thanking you for having the courage to speak up and asking for the information. Realizing that we don't know something important can make us feel powerless.

But we really aren't.

Enlightened ignorance is actually a really powerful place to be.

Learn to embrace it!

It is powerful because you have learned that there is something you need to know, and that in and of itself is knowledge. By embracing your enlightened ignorance, and asking for answers, you empower yourself and you continue to increase your knowledge and understanding of the topic at hand and your understanding of the world.

> An aside from Anne: I remember back in grade school – 6th grade to be exact – the smartest kid in the class was a boy I will refer to as J.R. He was smart and he knew it. The teachers knew it. We all knew it. So, when J.R. asked a question it was obviously a worthwhile question – he was a smart guy after all! What I remember most about J.R.'s questioning was his relentlessness in trying to get a satisfactory answer from the teacher, combined with his attitude, that I can best describe as "I need this information. I need you to do a better job of explaining it. You need to teach this so that I can understand it."
>
> J.R. embraced his Enlightened Ignorance, and came at the questioning from a place of empowerment. He knew he was a smart guy. He knew that he needed information. He demanded that information. I don't remember if he always got the information he sought......what I remember is that no one thought he was stupid for asking questions and expecting answers!

The concept of enlightened ignorance dates back at least to the ancient Greeks and is the basis for the Socratic method – a critical method of questioning that moves the questioner from a position of believing he or she knows something toward understanding truth. As we will discuss, this approach is a useful one and can be very powerful for emerging data practitioners.

Remember – this is an important and intellectually powerful place to be.

Your enlightened ignorance can serve as a catalyst for developing questions to help you better understand what you need to know. Furthermore, using your enlightened ignorance will sometimes help you recognize that the problem you're trying to solve may not be the problem that your dataset has identified. Or that the solution that you've developed is not reflective of the real-world challenge you're dealing with.

This is where the fun starts.

Enlightened ignorance is an empowered way to embrace the potential of that which we do not yet know and our desire to know it. It serves us better than the fear-based feelings of inadequacy and lack of knowledge experienced by so many people who suffer from data anxiety. We encourage people to use their enlightened ignorance to guide their search for knowledge – or truth, as Socrates would say.

Additionally, when we advocate for using enlightened ignorance, it includes the caveat that the information being requested should be delivered in a way that is easy to understand. Part of the power of enlightened ignorance is in the acknowledgment that not only is it acceptable not to know something; it is important to seek the necessary information without feeling ashamed or "less than" for not knowing.

What we mean by that is not allowing a so-called expert or data snob to intimidate you by using terms-of-art or highly technical language to explain a concept or a data set. Keep asking questions until they are answered – and answered in a way that you can understand. More often than not, this is easier than you think. Your continued questions may need to include phrases like: "can you explain that?" or "I don't understand that term – can you explain it?" or "what does _____ mean?" and our favorite "Can you use plain language when you explain that?"

In summary, enlightened ignorance is an important concept to embrace and can be an important component of your fear-fighting tool kit when you use it as a tool for learning. There are two ways that using your enlightened ignorance can become part of your fear-fighting tool kit:

1. Acknowledging that it is ok for you to not know things and using the need to know more as the first step in getting that information;
2. Legitimizing your requests for information to be presented in a straightforward manner, using plain language.

We will continue to reference enlightened ignorance often throughout this book because of its power to help you overcome your data fear.

Enlighted Ignorance Versus Analysis Paralysis: A Corollary

We just showed you how powerful understanding what you don't know but need to know can be. You don't want this to lead to data paralysis, however. And sometimes, there may be information that you need that you can't get right away. You may have to make a decision or take an action before you get that piece of information. Sometimes, not having the "right" or "full" information is used as an excuse not to use or analyze the data you have, to discount what the data you have might be showing you, or to "wait" (i.e., hang out in the analysis clothes dryer on spin cycle) until you get that proverbial "crucial piece of the puzzle."

Sometimes it is just not possible to have all the information you would like to have. We highly recommend not forgetting that there is important information you cannot access at the moment. (Mark Friedman calls this developing a "research agenda" and a "data development agenda.") However, when that is the case, and a decision has to be made or an action taken – we recommend using the BEST AVAILABLE data at the time. Many of us have seen decision processes be stuck in analysis long past the time when a decision was needed, either delaying the decision or making the analysis irrelevant (if the decision has already been made). We have also seen instances of people viewing reports of the best data that are available, and rather than trying to make use of the data, spending inordinate amounts of time identifying what is missing, or why the data don't tell us what we really need to know. As we indicated when we discussed enlightened ignorance, these are very important issues to bring up – you should never be afraid to ask "why?" or "what about?" However, such issues/questions should NOT, once mentioned, stop the decision team from using the best available data to inform their decision. There are always holes in the data, and data that we wish we could get are not available or not in an immediately analyzable or usable form.

Embracing enlightened ignorance is really about the empowerment of people who feel left out, less than, and intimidated to speak up and ask questions about data. Analysis paralysis is really about getting so deep into the questions and so deep into the search for the "right answer," or "perfect data set," that it stalls, inhibits, or paralyzes the completion of the work, thereby leaving the team with nothing.

These lead to another time when you shouldn't let NOT KNOWING something stop you from DOING something. Data science is a multi-dimensional, multi-disciplinary field with many different approaches, methods, statistical tests, etc. While we should strive always to keep learning and find out what we need to know...as we do that, we need to acknowledge that we may not have perfect information or perfect methods to complete the data task at hand. In these situations, we should USE WHAT WE KNOW and apply our practical problem-solving abilities. There is a lot you can do with simple tables, charts, and basic analysis (see Analysis Doesn't Have To Be Scary) while you are learning the vagaries of factor analysis, logistic regression analysis, and machine learning techniques.

What Do You Know That You Don't Know You Know?

This question was posed to Anne and her classmates many years ago by a professor in graduate school. At first, it seemed kind of silly and then a little "woo-woo," but in reality, this is a very powerful question, because it urges us to think about the knowledge we have that we take for granted, or don't even understand or realize exists.

We can look at this question in a couple of ways:

1. What are all the things we do that we don't think about? and/or
2. What knowledge do we have and use without consciously considering? Better stated: what is the body of knowledge that
   a) we have built up over the years, and regularly use without realizing it and
   b) which we can begin to harness when we understand and value it?

The first of these is easy to discuss and is interesting. It includes things like whether you remember the drive home from work each day, or whether you sometimes go on "auto-pilot" for certain stretches of highway, or when you are stuck at long traffic lights. It also includes remembering what you had for lunch on Wednesday or what you ate for dinner a couple of evenings ago. On some level, you know these things; you have done these things; and if you try hard enough, you can probably recall them. But you don't really pay attention to them because they don't matter to you.

The second kind of knowledge that we "don't know", or put more accurately – that we "don't credit ourselves as having", is the knowledge we have built up, sometimes over years, that allows us to do our jobs and perform complicated tasks – including data-related functions – that we don't even credit ourselves with knowing. If we continue to ignore this knowledge, we miss the opportunity to learn from ourselves – from past mistakes that taught us important lessons; from important experiences; and from tapping-in to a cache of information and skills we have developed over the years without realizing "what we know."

This is often a vast and often under-utilized reserve of knowledge and "know how" that we often rely on without even realizing it. We can draw on this "unacknowledged knowledge" or "personal knowledge bank" more if we begin to understand and value it.

We have discussed the ways that overcoming insecurities related to imposter syndrome, and harnessing our enlightened ignorance as an asset, helps us to continue developing both comfort and skills working with data. In a similar way, acknowledging, understanding, and crediting the knowledge and experience we already have can assist us in understanding that we have the capacity and ability to work with data. In fact, some of us may learn that we have been using our skills and working with data without realizing it.

So what do you really know?

Let's start by first reviewing what you already know and giving yourself credit for that knowledge. Then, we will discuss how to actually tap into that knowledge and actively put it to work for you.

The first step of this process is learning how to recognize, acknowledge, and appreciate the skills you already have. This process is quite simple. It is easy to gloss over and discount its importance.

Don't skip it.

Take the time to remember and honor your accomplishments and what you have learned. This isn't a "feel good" exercise; we will be using the results in the next step of the process.

Start by performing an inventory of your experiences, your skills, and projects you have worked on. Learn to tap into the things you have done and the lessons you have learned: actually read your resume and remember what you learned in the jobs you have held, the classes you have taken, and the degrees or certificates you have earned.

Here are some basic steps to performing the inventory, and you can add more if that makes sense for you:

1. Review your resume – actually read through it
    a. Review each job, or assignment, and what you actually did
    b. Ask yourself the following questions:
        i.) What skills did I learn or reinforce?
        ii.) What did I learn about what not to do?
    c. After reviewing each section, summarize your takeaway from that portion of your career or education. Write down the answers to the following questions:
        i.) How did it prepare me for my next step?
        ii.) How did it leave me stronger and more skilled?
        iii.) What did I learn about the strengths I bring to the table?
        iv.) What did I learn about the areas where I need more education, experience, or strength?
        v.) What did I learn about my department, organization, company, supervisor, etc., that I would change if I had the power, skills, experience, or authority to do so?
            1. Have you taken any steps to make that happen? If you have, make sure you include

this in your takeaway for that portion of your career or education

2. Learn about your skills and strengths by reviewing other people's information

   a. Review the resumes, LinkedIn pages, websites, blogs, etc., of your colleagues, supervisors, and mentors. (You can also look at those of someone you consider "the competition.")

      i.) Pay attention to the skills they credit themselves as having

      ii.) Ask yourself if you have performed the same tasks and activities

      iii.) Do you have the same skills and experiences with which they credit themselves?

   b. Review your takeaway summaries from your own resume

      i.) Add any skills and experiences that others have listed, and that make sense for you to list for yourself.

3. Recognize, acknowledge, and own the skills you already have! Each time you take on a new project, or start a new job, or learn something, you bring all of your skills and experiences with you. They make up the foundation on which you will continue to build. Appreciate all the things you already know!

The second step of the process is learning how to tap into skills you already have and utilizing your skills that can be applied from one type of work to another. We call these crossover skills. Consider:

Every time you approach a project or a challenge you bring what you know with you. How can you apply your vast – and growing – knowledge to current situations?

When beginning to understand and develop your crossover skills, you might not think your accounting skills, or facilitation skills, or project management skills, matter – but they really do. How can you apply these different skills in new situations?

How can you use your crossover skills in understanding data and reports?

How can you use your crossover skills in analyzing data and reports?

How you can use your outsider, or novice, status as a strength?

Notes

1 https://healthy.kaiserpermanente.org/health-wellness/health-encyclopedia/he.stress-management-breathing-exercises-for-relaxation.uz2255.
2 Developed by Meg Streams, PhD, Tennessee State University.
3 Kabat-Zinn, 1994, p. 4.
4 Guttman, R. The Hidden Power of Smiling; retrieved 02/02/2024 @ https://www.ted.com/talks/ron_gutman_the_hidden_power_of_smiling/transcript.
5 https://www.chabad.org/library/article_cdo/aid/2940/jewish/In-Pursuit-of-Ignorance.htm.

7

Analysis Doesn't Have to Be Scary

In this section, we will give you the opportunity to try out some of the data skills and relaxation techniques we have been writing about.

If we struggle with a fear of numbers and data, whether these fears are incapacitating or insidious and latent, they can be amplified when we are presented with a task where we not only have to compile, generate, calculate, or report data, but we also have to ANALYZE it. LOOK at all these numbers! LOOK at these charts! Your head can start to swivel back and forth, looking between different data displays and tables...your fears escalate, and you can decompensate and slink away, defeated.

Analysis doesn't have to be that way. Whether we are looking at numeric data or other kinds of information about our world, we are trying to do some basic things: describe, understand and explain, and, sometimes, predict. If we think about looking at the data we are working with as simply trying to do these basic tasks, we can find comfort in that.

In any analysis sequence, the first thing we do is understand what we have to work with. Think of a crime scene investigation (we have all seen CSI or NCIS, haven't we?). The first thing our intrepid investigators do is gather evidence (what CAN the crime scene tell us?). Is there a murder weapon? Can the body give us a clue about the manner of death? What about the time of death? Is there other evidence? Fingerprints? DNA/blood

DOI: 10.4324/9781003496328-11

evidence? Spent shell casings? Bullets lodged in walls? Evidence of a struggle? Is the body identified? This creates an inventory of what the investigators have to work with. This information is first used to DESCRIBE what they think happened. In the same way, data analysis starts with an assessment of the data that are available for analysis and describes those data through things like frequency distributions, measure of central tendency (e.g., averages), and basic charts like histograms (which show data distributed in ranges), pie, line, and bar. These data help us to describe what is happening with the phenomena, events, activities, programs, organizations, policies, or systems about which we have collected data. In building a "first approximation" description of what we are examining, we bring disparate elements together to build a holistic picture of what we are seeing. So, we look to these basic ways of looking at distributions and other basic data visualizations to help us build a holistic picture.

Data Meditation: Measures of Central Tendency

Concept

One common way we tend to summarize data is to report an average or "measure of central tendency." This can be the actual, arithmetic average (e.g., if the data series is 1, 2, 3, then $1 + 2 + 3 = 6$, divided by the number of observations (3), equals an average of 2. Another measure of central tendency that is often used is the median, where half the values in a data series are above that number and half are below (1, 2, 3) – median =2. A third measure of central tendency is the mode – the most frequently occurring value in a data series (e.g., 1, 1, 2, 3) – mode =1 [if there is no recurring value in a data series, such a 1, 2, 3, the data series is said to be "modeless"] ☺.

The measure of central tendency you select to report can be important. Arithmetic averages can be highly influenced by extreme values. For instance, if you have a data series that is 1, 1, 1, 1, 1, and 10, the arithmetic average would equal 6.5…which would be a very misleading summary of the data series. Both the median and the mode, on the other hand, = 1, which is a much better representation of the "central tendency" in the data.

Example

We often see this in reports that examine income. *Median income* is used rather than average income (or even modal income) because there are many situations with a few individuals with very low or very high incomes that can inflate, or deflate, average income. This problem is avoided if median income is used. Please see the example below. In this example, the median is clearly the most meaningful measure of central tendency for this data series. The average is inflated by the extremely high values, and, because there are only two recurring values, the mode is anchored to a very low value. Median wins! (Table 7.1).

Let's Meditate...

Other than income data, think about data that you use (or could use) in your work. Are there times when you might use a measure of central tendency other than the arithmetic average? For what reason?

TABLE 7.1 Mean vs. Median Example

$11,000	
$11,000	
$12,000	
$17,500	
$19,500	
$21,000	
$22,000	
$65,000	
$75,000	
Average	$27,400
Median	$19,500
Mode	$11,000

Source: Created by the authors.

Data Meditation: Distributions and Variability

When Ron teaches statistics to graduate students, he has found that they do ok with frequency tables (see counting and categorizing meditation) and measures of central tendency (see measures of central tendency meditation), but when he starts talking about how data are distributed, and how much variation is observed in data, students can get that "deer in headlights" look. One reason might be that the term normal curve starts to be used, and students can have a visceral reaction to anything called a curve. Another reason is that when we examine variability, we start using terms like variance and standard deviation, and along with these terms come **FORMULAS.** They are not very complex, but they do contain some features that may not have been encountered by students before.

Distributions

A distribution is a collection of observations for a particular measure (or variable) of interest, viewed by appropriate value ranges. The chart below shows unemployment rates for service areas for an employment and training program. Notice the NORMAL curve imposed over the data, which, while not EXACTLY normal, is essentially normal. A normal curve is a probability distribution. It is a graph where the data cluster around the mean, with the highest frequency in the center, and gradually decrease toward the tails. This normal distribution is often described as a bell curve because it has the general shape of a bell. It is called normal because many continuous variables in nature have this kind of distribution. The key to understanding this is thinking about what central tendency implies…when data are exactly normal, the mean, median, and mode are all equivalent. That means the mean is the most frequently occurring value (the centerline and peak of the normal distribution) and less frequent values are arrayed around it, with ever-decreasing frequencies (Figure 7.1).

One of the things students are uncomfortable about is the notion that a normal curve has certain characteristics, but in practice almost no data are completely normal. Yet, in many cases we

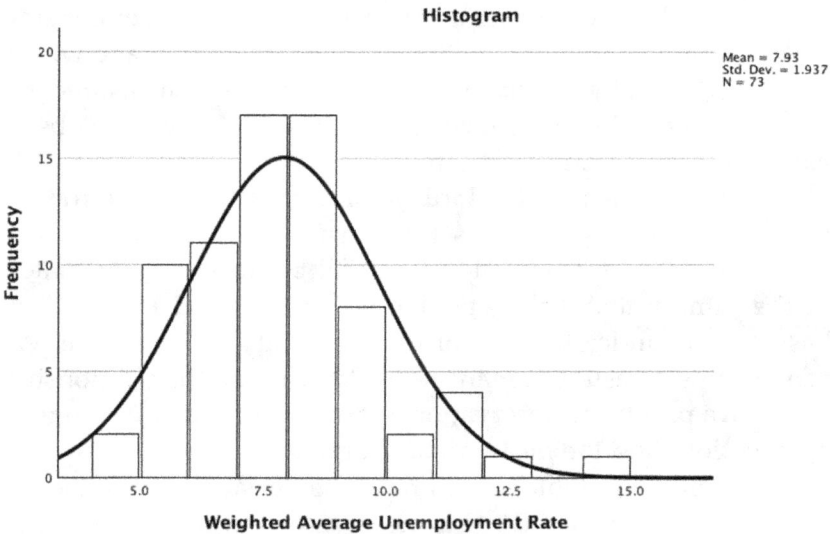

FIGURE 7.1 Normal curve example. Note: Mean = 7.93, Std. Dev. = 1.937, N = 73. *Source:* Created by the authors.

go on to ignore that the data are not completely normal and treat them as if they are normal. More on that later.

There are reasons why normality is so important. Normal curves are symmetrical (if you folded a normal curve on its center line, the two halves of the curve would match up, kind of like a butterfly) and have certain important characteristics. One important characteristic is called the "empirical rule," which we will talk about shortly – once we have discussed the important concept of variability.

Variability

In an earlier data meditation, we explored measures of central tendency, including the arithmetic average or mean. In a normal curve, the mean is the centerline of the normal curve. However, not all normal curves look the same. Some have high peaks, some are flatter. Some have long tails, some don't. The shape of the normal curve depends on the relationship of the individual data points (observations) to the mean – or how much they vary from the mean. Sometimes most of the data are not very far from the mean, tending to make the curve tall and narrow. Sometimes most of the data are further away from the mean, on either side of the mean. This would tend to make the curve flatter and wider.

This dispersion of data around the mean is measured by something called **variance**, which measures how far each observation in a set is from the mean.

Another measure, **standard deviation,** is the square root of the variance and is a very useful measure of dispersion around the mean. Standard deviation is useful because it is calculated in the same units of the variable of interest, and it forms the basis of our understanding of the variability of a variable. We can use this measure in many ways to examine the relationship between a particular observation, set of observations, or range of observations and the mean of that variable.

The following table shows how the variance and standard deviation are calculated for a measure of the number of days students brought their lunch to school. As you can see, the variance is straightforward to calculate, but hard to interpret, while the standard deviation is more useful; it shows that while the mean number of days students took their lunch to school was 7.8, there is substantial variability within this data set, and the average amount individual counts varied from 7.8 was 5.05 (Table 7.2).

The actual formula for variance is as follows:

$$s^2 = \frac{\Sigma(x_i - \bar{x})^2}{n-1}$$

where the sample variance (25.5 in the table) is equal to the sum of the differences in each observation from the mean (e.g., the difference for the number of times Paul brought his lunch (5) from the average, 7.8), squared (356.4), and then divided by the number of observations (15) −1 (14). When said it in words, the formula doesn't seem so scary, does it?

In our example of unemployment rates for service delivery areas, the average unemployment rate was 7.91%. However, the average distance from the mean, measured by standard deviation, was 1.97%. That means, on average, scores were two points higher or lower than the mean. You can see that without

TABLE 7.2 Variation from the Mean

Student	Number of Times They Brought Lunch from Home in Last 30 Days	Difference from Mean	Squared Difference from Mean
Paul	5	−2.8	7.84
Lucy	3	−4.8	23.04
Devin	9	1.2	1.44
George	12	4.2	17.64
Lisa	7	−0.8	0.64
Laura	6	−1.8	3.24
Aaron	0	−7.8	60.84
Jeff	19	11.2	125.44
Kate	4	−3.8	14.44
Lorelei	2	−5.8	33.64
Jennifer	11	3.2	10.24
Pete	14	6.2	38.44
Sven	9	1.2	1.44
Gunter	11	3.2	10.24
Heidi	5	−2.8	7.84
Mean	7.8		
		Sum of Squared Differences	**356.4**
		Divided by Number of Observations Minus 1	**25.5**
		Variance	**25.5**
		Standard Deviation (Square Root of Variance)	**5.05**

Source: Created by the authors.

standard deviation, it is difficult to understand what is going on with distribution or to interpret the mean appropriately. Standard deviation helps us understand how informative the mean is... generally, the more dispersion in the data, the less useful the mean is, by itself.

Getting back to the normal curve, the "empirical rule," or the "68–95–99.7" rule, states that in a normal distribution, 68% of the observations will fall within one standard deviation of the mean, 95% of the observations will fall within two standard deviations of the mean, and 99.7% of the observation will fall within three standard deviations from the mean. This rule is very helpful and can help the analyst understand just how far away a particular value or set of values is from the mean. Using something called **z-score**, you can calculate EXACTLY how far away from the mean a particular observation is, in standard deviation units.

Ultimately, this framework (distance from the mean, measured in standard deviation units) is then used to determine whether a particular observation is significantly different from the mean, which is a foundational concept in data analysis. The specifics are too elaborate to discuss here, but knowing that all of that "significance stuff" is fundamentally about where on the normal curve an observation falls can make this mysterious process much less daunting.

There are many different distributions depending on the type of data you are examining. A normal curve is utilized when examining continuous data, or data that can take on an infinite number of values within a given range. However, there are many variables for which this is not true, such as for a variable with only two allowable values. The following chart shows the distribution of values for a variable that counts the number of individuals within a program who are Hispanic or Latino and those who are not. This is called a dichotomous variable. ANOTHER WEIRD TERM! You can see how the language used, and these distinctions, get peoples' heads spinning! (Figure 7.2).

Data Deconstruction

As we all know, while description is laudable, it doesn't get us very far. We want to understand and explain what we are investigating. This is where we start to DECONSTRUCT our holistic description of what we see with the data, into components, or smaller chunks, that may help us better understand what we are seeing.

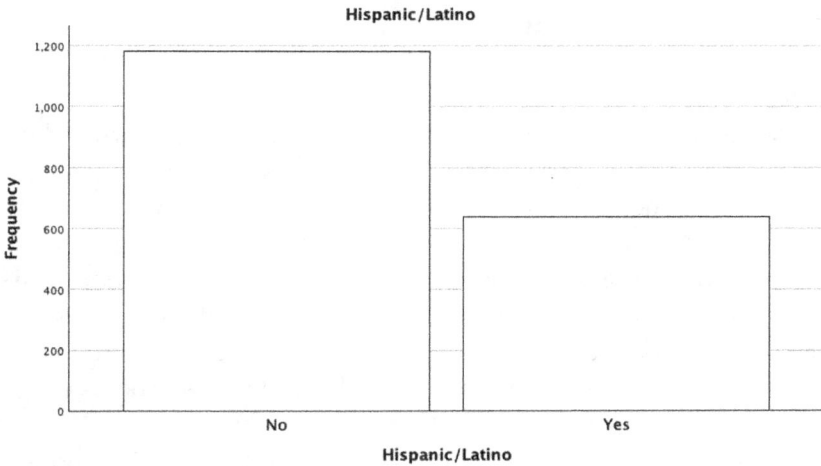

FIGURE 7.2 Dichotomous variable example. *Source:* Created by the authors.

The notion of analysis as deconstruction is not a new one. The Cambridge Dictionary of Philosophy defines analysis as "The process of breaking up a concept, proposition, linguistic complex, or fact into its simple or ultimate constituents,"[1] or, in other words, breaking down the information into its most basic parts. Going all the way back to Aristotle, analysis has been defined in similar fashion. Immanuel Kant combines two senses of analysis in his work, one derived from Greek geometry and the other from modern physics and chemistry. Both remain close to the original Greek sense of analysis as "loosening up" or "releasing," but each proceeds in different ways. The former proceeds by assuming a proposition to be true and *searching for another known truth from which the proposition may be deduced.* The latter proceeds by resolving complex wholes into their elements.[2]

One way we deconstruct data is to categorize it, breaking all of the observations into categories. We usually start this using the Sesame Street method – "which of these things is not like the other," sorting observations into groups with finer and finer degrees of discernment. This way, we can disaggregate observations into different groups.

Data Meditation: Disaggregation

Concept

We talked about measures of central tendency in our earlier data meditation. In this data meditation, we consider that even when a particular measure of central tendency is reflective of a data series, *it may not be telling the whole story*.

We often aggregate (combine) data across different individual units, like different programs, different program sites, or different geographical jurisdictions (like catchment areas, counties, or states). We then report these data as "the average outcome for a program is X" or the "statewide average is Y."

Sometimes, however, these aggregations do not reflect important features of the data. There may be a wide variation in an outcome measure by program location...or in a statewide measure for members of a particular sub-population. Reporting just the average in these cases misses an important aspect of the story.

Example

Consider the example of chronic absenteeism rates. The overall rate of chronic absenteeism for Connecticut is 10%. However, the rate for City Hartford is 50%. Examining the Hartford data at an even more granular level, the rate of chronic absenteeism for Hispanics is over 70%. This is an example of multiple levels of aggregation masking the extent or seriousness of a disturbing data trend.

Let's Meditate....

If you saw a trend in state graduation rates like the one shown below, what questions would you have? What kinds of disaggregation might reflect part of an otherwise hidden story (Figure 7.3)?

Cross-Tabulation

One of the simple tools we often use to disaggregate data is cross-tabulation. In its simplest form, cross-tabulation just

Four Year High School Graduation Rate

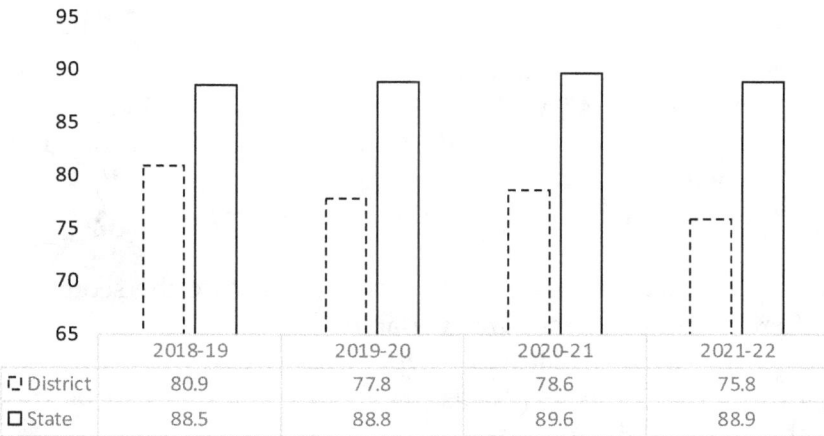

	2018-19	2019-20	2020-21	2021-22
District	80.9	77.8	78.6	75.8
State	88.5	88.8	89.6	88.9

FIGURE 7.3 Disaggregation example. *Source:* Created by the authors.

TABLE 7.3 Cross-Tabulation Example

	Not Justice Involved	Justice Involved	Total
Male	30	45	75
Female	60	32	92
Total	90	77	167

Source: Created by the authors.

breaks overall total counts of two variables, each with only two categories, into cells where we see how many share specific cross-categories (things in common).

Cross-Tabulation Example[3]

In the table, there are 167 program participants, 77 of whom are justice involved. Of those justice involved, 45 are male and 32 are female. A higher percentage of the male participants are justice involved, even though there are more female participants overall. Clearly, we can learn a lot from a simple disaggregation, not involving higher math (Table 7.3).

Notice that while we deconstructed the data in the above example, our simple analysis entailed comparing the different groups. Many contend that comparison is the essence of analysis.

Even when we deconstruct, we often deconstruct in order to
COMPARE:

♦ We compare different individuals on the same variables
♦ we compare variables with themselves over time
♦ we compare the same measures for the same program
   delivered at different geographies
♦ or the same measures for similar programs.

When we break things into groups, we compare the scores for
different groups on the same variables.

This is the foundation of hypothesis testing – we are comparing what we expect to see if our hypothesis might be true
with the NULL hypothesis...we are "disconfirming the null."

Remembering this logic of comparison is important. It can
settle you down when you are looking at a bunch of data. Keeping
in mind that making these critical comparisons in what you are
trying to do can help. Taking this approach, the data won't seem
as random, or like a bunch of big indistinct ink blots. Rather,
approaching the data in a systematic way, working our way to
deconstruction and comparison, can feel liberating.

Another thing we often do to understand and explain is
to try to discern patterns. PATTERN RECOGNITION is also a
kind of comparison. When we look for patterns, we compare
instances to see if they are similar, over time or for different
groups. A specific kind of pattern recognition is looking for
COVARIATION, which is when two variables do or don't
move together. When we look to see whether two variables
move together (or don't), and whether one is increasing as the
another does (positive correlation) or one is increasing as the
other decreases (negative correlation), we are essentially comparing the two variables over time or across our units of analysis (Figure 7.4).

The above example shows a very definite correlation between
the percentage of participants employed at exit and the recidivism rate (the rate of committing new crimes). There is more to
do (see below), but this is a starting point.

Covariation Example

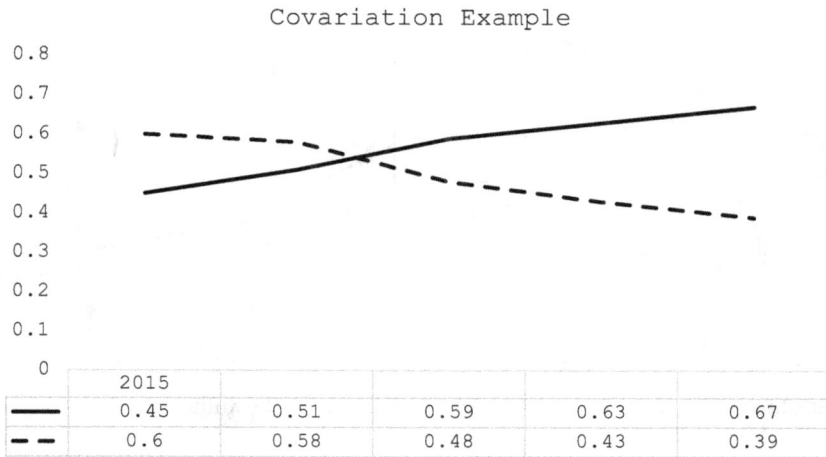

	2015				
——	0.45	0.51	0.59	0.63	0.67
– –	0.6	0.58	0.48	0.43	0.39

FIGURE 7.4 Covariation example. *Source:* Created by the authors.

If we are data-traumatized, it is easy to recoil from terms like hypothesis testing, covariation, or correlation. But if we understand that all we are really talking about is different kinds of comparison, and we approach it in a common sense, practical way, this can ease our fears.

We are often trying to engage in understanding cause (causal reasoning) when we are trying to explain what we are seeing. When we think about cause and effect, we employ all of the tools described above. First, let's get one thing out of the way – usually we are not going so far as to PROVE cause and effect. You have probably heard the maxim "correlation is not causation." Just because two variables move together does not mean one causes the other. This is clearly often not the case. But we use both of those types of observations…observing variables moving together, and observing WHEN things occur, to get us closer to understanding what might be contributing to what we are seeing (or the problems we are trying to solve). We chart data for different variables together, in dual line charts (charts that show two different lines of data) or in scatter plots (scatterplots use dots to represent values for two different numeric variables. The position of each dot on the horizontal and vertical axes indicates values for an individual data point.[4]), to see whether there is

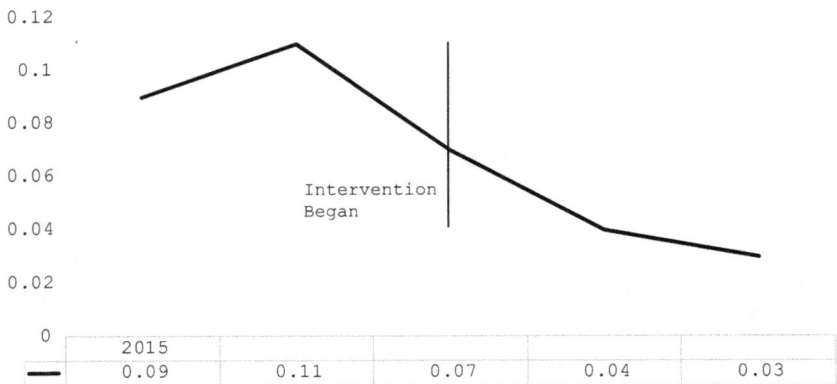

	2015				
▬	0.09	0.11	0.07	0.04	0.03

FIGURE 7.5 Times-series example. *Source:* Created by the authors.

covariation. If we are trying to see whether some intervention is working, we look at what happened BEFORE the intervention and then what happened AFTER (Figure 7.5).

Take a look at the chart above: The "x" axis (running along the bottom) shows a number of years (a time sequence). In the above example, a program aimed at reducing the percentage of youth involved in the justice system, which is shown in the "y" (or vertical) axis, started at the beginning of 2017, and there is a clear, multi-year decrease in the justice involvement rate post-intervention.

That is the simple case. However…as analysts we have to be careful. While these data are encouraging, just because the rate decreased following the intervention does not demonstrate that the intervention CAUSED the rate decrease.

There could be other interventions happening simultaneously, or there could be other factors, like an improved economy, which might have something to do with the rate decrease. Looking at these factors would be the next step in the analysis…But this is a good starting point.

Data Meditation: Trend Analysis

Trend Analysis (Figure 7.6)

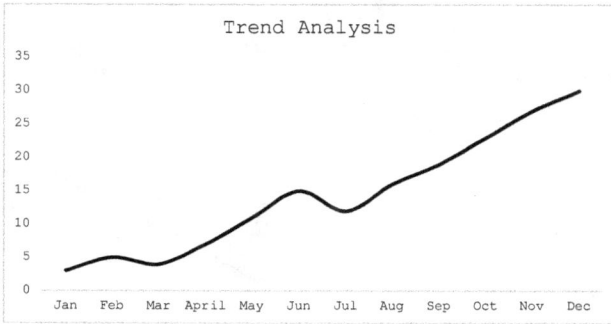

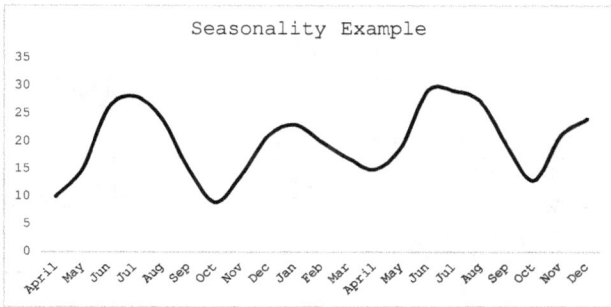

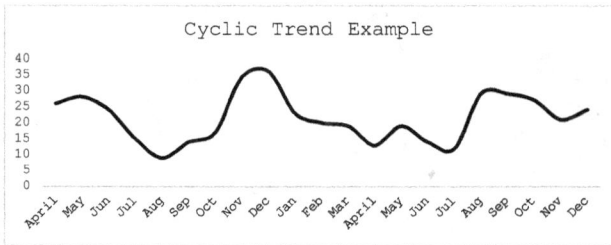

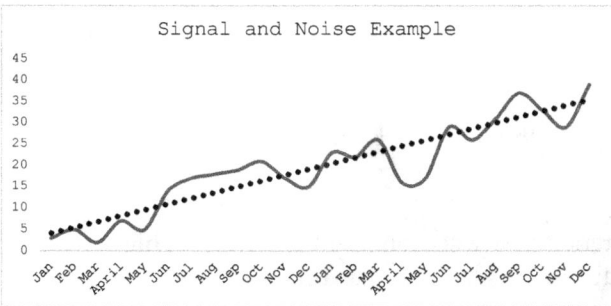

FIGURE 7.6 Trend examples. *Source:* Created by the authors.

Trend Analysis

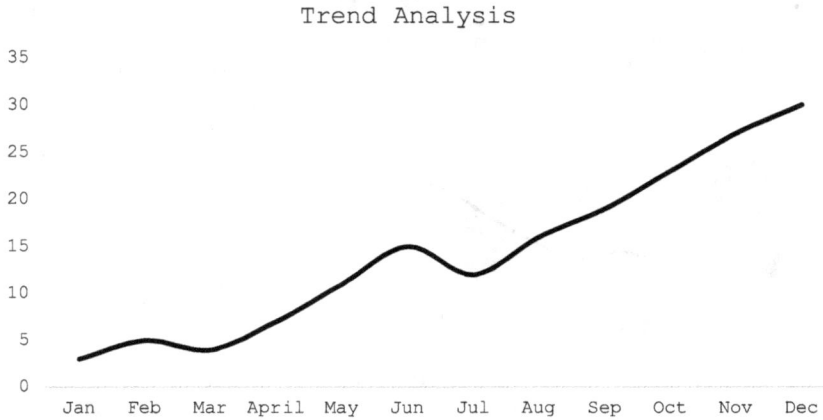

FIGURE 7.6A Trend example.

Some trends are straightforward, and it is easy to see the direction and magnitude of change over time.

Seasonality Example

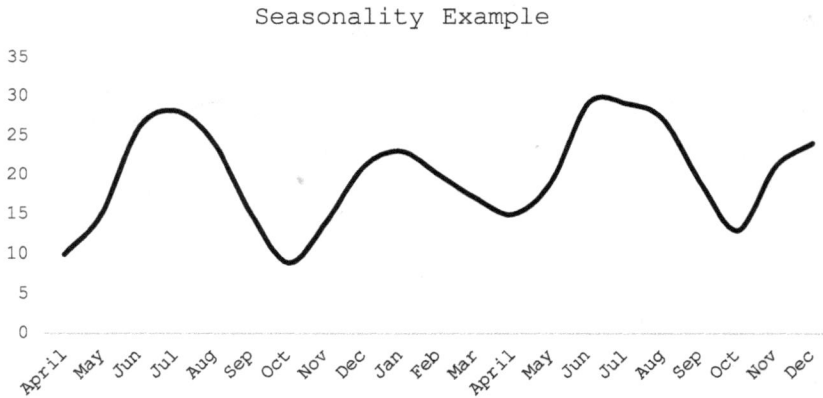

FIGURE 7.6B Seasonality example.

Some trends have a seasonal component, like higher employment levels during the summer vacation and Christmas seasons.

Cyclic Trend Example

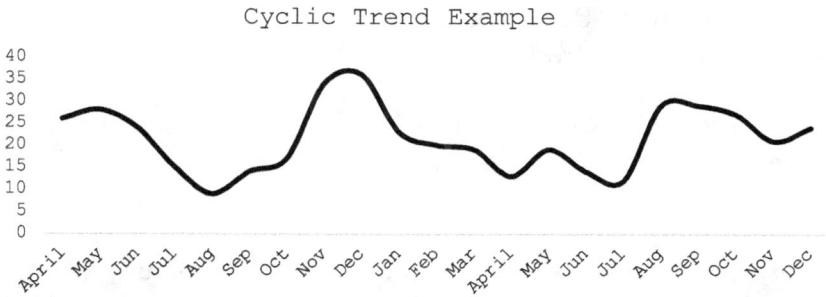

FIGURE 7.6C Cyclic trend.

Some trends have cyclic components, where the same dynamic occurs over and over again, but is not necessarily tied to time period or season.

Signal and Noise Example

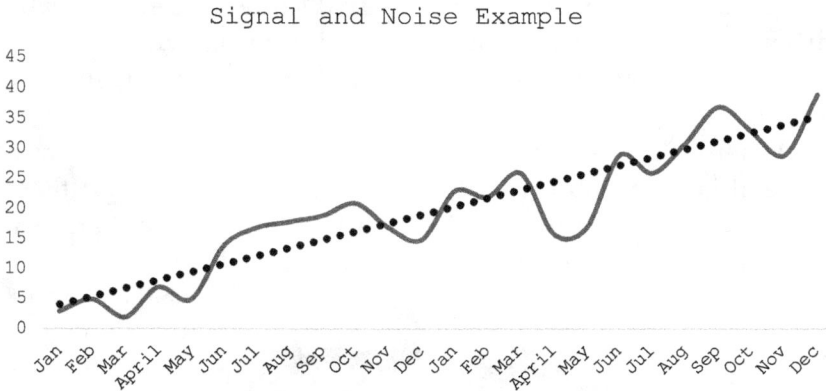

FIGURE 7.6D Signal and noise example.

Some trends have a lot of incidental variation, or noise, but once the noise is removed the essential trend can be revealed. The key is to "see the signal through the noise," trying to understand the variation you are seeing and the implications for the phenomena you are analyzing.

As we try to deconstruct what we are seeing with such observations, we introduce new variables that might include:

◆ individual demographics or risk factors,
◆ other trends that are occurring during our periods of observation,
◆ differences in geography,
◆ or differences in the components or nature of the intervention.

What we are trying to do here is understand how much of the variation in our variable of interest (percentage of youth involved in the justice system) we are seeing is due to the cause or causes we suspect are having effect – the 2017 intervention. And we are looking at the other potential variables mentioned to reduce the possibility that the cause-and-effect relationship we think we are observing is not real – that something else is really driving the variation. We are also looking to see whether other factors are impacting the primary cause-and-effect sequence we are observing.

When we look at multiple things that impact an out-come, it is called multivariate examination. We can build these examinations of multiple variables into models, which can then help us PREDICT future events (Figure 7.7).

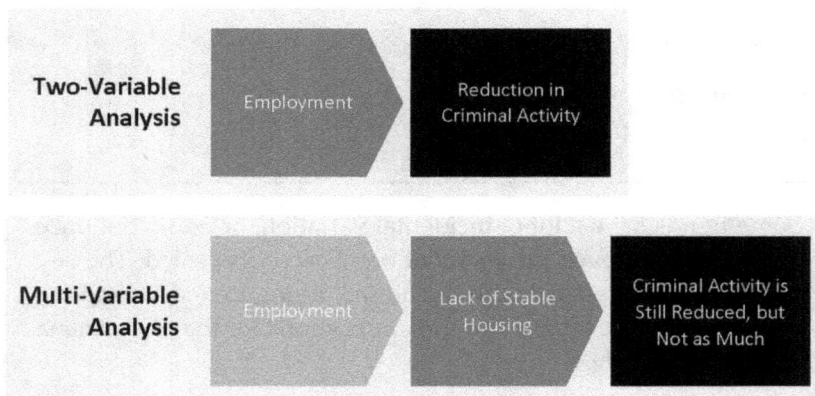

FIGURE 7.7 Multivariate example. *Source:* Created by the authors.

In the example above, the lack of stable housing moderates the positive effect of employment on potential recidivism. There still is a relationship between employment and reduced recidivism rates, but it is not as strong for those who do not have stable housing. We would not know this if we did not include the "stable housing" variable in the analysis.

Of course, it is easy to get carried away with introducing new variables into the analysis...we can become paralyzed by fear that we have not included something that might be important (remember our earlier discussion on analysis paralysis). We should use two important principles to guide us here...one, called "Occam's Razor," says that we should not add more elements into models than necessary[5]...in other words, the simplest models that capture a high proportion of the variation we are seeing is best. The second is the notion of "Satisficing,"[6] which is a recognition that we humans (and even our machine models) have "bounded rationality." While we would like our models to be absolutely comprehensive and explain all the variation we are seeing, this is usually not possible...so we make do with models that that "satisfice," or are "good enough." Remember these principles can make our model building, prediction, and analysis efforts less desperate and can help us break free from "analysis paralysis."

This kind of discussion can make people experiencing data fear begin to feel woozy ☺. But there is a real benefit to understanding that in the end, we are still just looking at information: first one variable at a time, then one variable disaggregated in different ways, and then multiple variables together, in a SEQUENCE or COMBINATION OF COMPARISONS. Plain, old, comparisons. The underlying math just facilitates and quantifies these comparisons, but comparisons remain.

The Gift that Keeps on Giving

Once you have identified what you fear and used some of our basic tools to address your fear, you will likely find that you have decreased your level of anxiety about using data, and you may have even changed where you sit on the data-comfort scale.

Let's do a quick review of some of what we have discussed to this point:

Relax and center: When encountering the need to work with data, breathe deeply and get oxygen to your brain. Remember, much of data work is not complex number crunching, but applying common sense in order to understand something. You can handle this.

Bust your anxiety: Use one of our anxiety busters – or create your own steps to busting your anxiety.

Anne's anxiety-busting steps include:

♦ Recognizing that I am feeling anxious and beginning to spiral down into stinking thinking about my abilities. I also recognize that I am empowered to take control of the narrative in my head and change the messages I am giving myself from negative to positive

♦ Breathing intentionally so that I can get oxygen into my brain so that I can think better, and be more objective instead of fear-driven

♦ Centering myself and calling on my higher power so that I can get out of the flight-or-fight response and create the presence of mind that allows me to remember what I know and to use that knowledge to address the data challenge

♦ Remembering that I know what I know and that I can use the knowledge I have to tackle the problem at hand. Instead of doubting my knowledge and experience, I can use it to help me understand and analyze the situation at hand. It is part of my strength

♦ Reviewing the situation with my empowered frame of mind. I will ask myself basic questions that help me assess the situation in an objective, calm, and confident way

♦ Dissecting the task, problem, or assignment into smaller tasks or questions that are easier to answer or analyze, while remembering to keep those deep, calming breaths coming

◆ Reinforcing my belief that I can handle the challenge and that any problems may not be related to me or my skills, but that there may be a flaw in the assignment, task, or piece of information I am encountering, or that I may need to review my steps to make sure I am not missing something

◆ Asking for help if the problem is still vexing me, or if I need someone with more data experience to help me decode a document. I use my enlightened ignorance, remembering that asking questions and learning something new are both powerful and are ways to increase my knowledge

Ron's Anxiety Buster includes:

◆ Making sure not to ignore data qualms, and acknowledging the signals my mind is sending

◆ Breathing and taking a few moments to center myself, and trying to get the rational part of my brain working again

◆ Identifying the danger (what IS it that I am afraid of) to understand what I am afraid might happen, and understanding the essential risk underlying our fear, such as misinterpretation of data; uncertainty about what someone might do with the data; being blamed for poor data quality or poor performance; losing resources or feeling embarrassed at poor performance

◆ Acknowledging that risk is often real and there is always something I can do to manage and mitigate any risk

◆ Developing a risk management approach that includes developing a risk management strategy based on the perceived risk

◆ *Getting a little help from my friends* when I have trouble identifying an appropriate risk mitigation strategy on my own. Sometimes it is just a question of talking through the risk with someone who has experience with a similar circumstance or issue. Sometimes, in order to implement a specific risk management approach, one may need to surmount other technical issues. Here, I might run into fears related to my own capacity related to those technical issues. Asking friends for help – and by extension, getting additional technical assistance or training...is important here

♦ Understanding that the fear that I might actually VOICE is NOT really the fear that I am actually EXPERIENCING. Being mindful of this back at the fear acknowledgment stage, and being honest about what I am really afraid of, helps to act accordingly

Move toward Your Fear: Understanding our data fears and actually addressing them, instead of hiding from them, is the same as dealing with most other kinds of fears. Realizing that by standing up to the fear monster, and looking it straight in the eye, we strip the monster of its power over us. By acknowledging and addressing our fears, we empower ourselves to move past the fear and acknowledge our strengths, forgive our weaknesses, learn the skills we need, and ask for help when that is needed.

Use Your Enlightened Ignorance: Enlightened ignorance is the state we enter when we realize that we are missing a piece of information, or we don't have some kind of knowledge that we need.

Enlightened ignorance can empower us in two specific ways:

1. Acknowledging that it is ok not to know things and using the need to know more as the first step in getting that information.
2. Legitimizing requests for information to be presented in a straightforward manner, using plain language.

Bring Your Own Experience to Bear: We carry with us the knowledge we have built up, sometimes over years, that allows us to do our jobs, and perform complicated tasks, including data-related functions that we don't even credit ourselves with knowing. In short, we know a lot more than we sometimes realize. Every time we address a problem, solve an equation, or make a judgment, we bring this body of knowledge with us. Tap into that knowledge and start to consciously harvest some of what you know when you are solving problems and creating solutions.

Deconstruct the Process of Analysis into Bite-Sized Pieces

Analysis can seem intimidating if you don't break it down into bite-sized pieces. Those pieces include:

♦ **Describe:** Data analysis starts with an assessment of the data that are available for the analysis and describes those data through things like averages and basic charts
♦ **Deconstruct:** Deconstruct the data by breaking it into components, or smaller chunks, that may help us better understand what we are seeing. This can include categorizing the data and also disaggregating the data.
♦ **Compare:** We then compare the data – perhaps by different categories and perhaps after disaggregating it.
♦ **Recognize Patterns:** We look for patterns, which includes comparing instances to see if they are similar, over time or for different groups.
♦ **Make Predictions:** We look at multiple things that impact an outcome and can build these examinations into models, which can then help us predict future events.

There is a real benefit to understanding that when we conduct analyses, we are still just looking at information, first one variable at a time, then one variable disaggregated in different ways, and then multiple variables together, in a sequence or combination of comparisons. Plain, old, comparisons. The underlying math just facilitates and quantifies these comparisons, but comparisons remain.

See What You Can See

The gift that keeps on giving is the gift you give yourself when you invest in understanding your fears, you find a way to bust your anxiety, you learn the power of enlightened ignorance, and you learn that analysis doesn't have to be scary. All of these steps lead to your realization that you can use data and help to vanquish the fear monster.

You have gained a sense of control over data, and you realize that data don't have to be a four-letter word; instead, you can harness the power of data to help you understand your world and your work.

Data Meditation: . . . Interpreting a Multivariate Data Display

Sometimes, encountering a complex data display or data table can provoke a visceral fear response. Sometimes, the response can be so intense that you may feel like running screaming from the room. Even if you resist the temptation, a complex data display can cause anxiety and can cause you to avoid engaging with the display. This may be an unfortunate loss, because many of these displays offer insights not easily experienced with narrative or other approaches to information transfer.

Let's get relaxed before we view anxiety-provoking data:

- ◆ Stop and breathe
- ◆ Self-affirmation – I can do this
- ◆ Focus: attack the fear monster and address the data
- ◆ Calm the whirlwind of fear and uncertainty
- ◆ See the data for what it is
- ◆ Decode and deconstruct
- ◆ End up with key takeaway

Consider the following data display:

Some people, when viewing the above data displays, would immediately dismiss it as too complex, or think the equivalent of, "what the hell is this?" and move on without engaging with the information contained in the display. An important step in the data-comfort journey is to resist this, and rather than avoiding

Risky Behaviors, 2019

(a)

Risky Behaviors, 2021

(b)

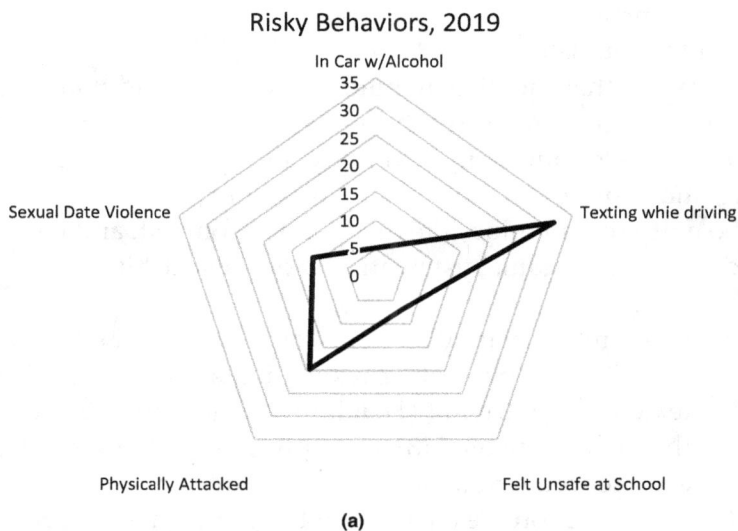

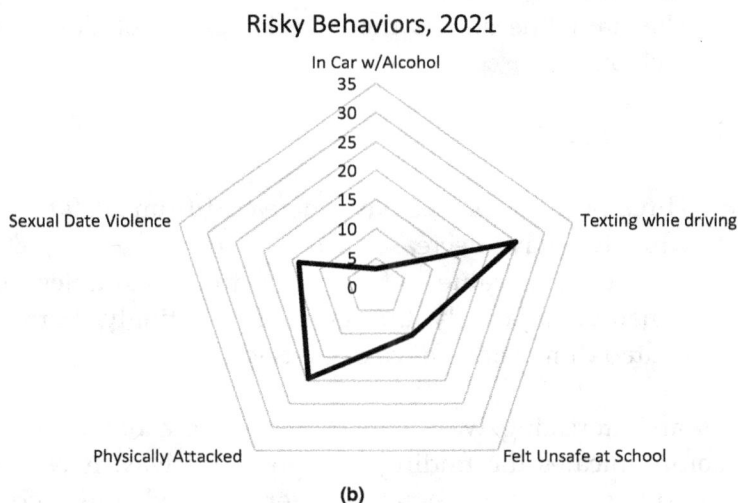

FIGURE 7.8 Complex chart example. *Source:* Created by the authors.

the data, to move toward the data and engage with the display (Figure 7.8).

Be mindful that the display has the potential to produce (or is already producing) data anxiety.

Take a breath.

Center yourself.

Consider that the display might have value and that maybe, just maybe, you can approach the data the way you would any problem you encounter in your daily life – practically, systematically, and confident that you can work it out.

So, with that in mind, Breathe! Center yourself, and consider the data display again. Systematically deconstruct it…

◆ How many variables can you identify? Let's see…it has ..5 – the percent of respondents that reported they texted while driving (1), felt unsafe at school (2), were in the car with alcohol (3), were physically attacked (4), and experienced sexual date violence (5)

◆ The spines on the chart show the percentage reported for each of those variables

◆ The dark line shows these variables in relationship to each other

So what do we see?

◆ Three of the variables have increased from 2019 to 2021, while two have decreased

◆ The relative values of each of these variables have remained relatively the same. Interestingly, both car-related dimensions have decreased.

This is an interesting way to experience these data, and one that communicates the finding in a powerful way. It was also NOT hard to see, once we breathed, were focused, and used our everyday deconstruction skills to identify the components of the display and what the display was doing.

Of course, there are many data displays (and even complex data tables) that are much more complex and would require much more deconstruction and systematic review. However, the process is still the same, and unless a data display is poorly designed, or flawed in some way, even very complex displays can be tackled in this manner. Just remember to use any anxiety busters that work for you as you approach the display, and be confident in your awareness that you will be able to pull apart the display to better understand it. Don't let the threatening initial impression or impact of the display prevent you from putting your big-kid pants on and successfully engaging with the display ☺

The Agonies and the Ecstasies of Data Visualizations and Data

One of the "sexier" aspects of data work is the use of data visualizations and data dashboards. Data visualizations can be a powerful addition to the analyst toolbox. When used effectively, they can help data users see data patterns and relationships in a clear, meaningful way, often much more quickly than more prosaic forms of data reporting. As data become more accessible, and data visualization tools become easier to use, it has become much easier to create data visualizations and data dashboards. However, it is important to understand several risks associated with creating and using these "wow factor" devices.

Data visualization supports, but does not REPLACE, data analysis. As a new data practitioner, that means you need to understand that consideration of the data – by you – is necessary, including thinking about what the visualization is actually showing (and what it isn't showing) and whether it seems accurate and makes sense. What questions does the visualization prompt in your mind? What do you still need to know?

Data visualizations, like so many other things, are subject to "garbage in, garbage out." If the source data are bad, so is the data visualization…even if it is pretty ☺

In the same way that not all good-looking people are good people, not all good-looking data displays are displaying good data. As a new data practitioner, you can feel comfortable asking about the data sources for a data visualization you have been asked to view. If you need to perform work based on the data represented in the visualization, make sure you will be able to see the underlying data and have the ability to go through the steps in our "Data Analysis Doesn't Have to be Scary" section.

Data visualizations, and data dashboards, are often a kind of data aggregation. Whenever you aggregate data, you can lose information. Some interactive data visualizations and data dashboards support "drilling down" into the data shown in initial, summary displays...but even with drill downs information may be lost (especially if the drilldowns are selective, which is often the case with complex data sets). This can lead to misinterpretation of the data. Intentional and unintentional data selectivity can lead to incorrect conclusions and mistrust of data.

In the same way that averages don't tell the real story, aggregated data lose important information about specific data sets within the larger, aggregated data that you may see in a data visualization. One example of this is chronic absenteeism data displayed for all Connecticut children. When the data were aggregated for all children, there was a 15% rate of chronic absenteeism. However, when the data were disaggregated by race, ethnicity, and family income, rates varied from 12% for some groups to 26% for others. This significant difference between groups told a very different story and suggested different approaches, than the aggregated rate for all children.

Similar to aggregations, disaggregating the data can also cause you to lose some information. By focusing on only part of the data instead of all the data, it is possible to lose sight of the larger data set and to take the disaggregated data out of context. As you can see from the previous paragraph, we believe that disaggregating data can be very useful; the message here is that it is important to remember to contextualize the disaggregated data within the larger data set.

Just like any data being reviewed or analyzed, it is important to understand the data that are being used to create the visualization or dashboard. Unfortunately, because they are visual and often compelling, the display dazzles the viewer, and many viewers do not take the next step to really understand the data being shown. When produced correctly, any such displays will also provide access to the metadata that provide explanations of the sources and nature of the data elements used to create the displays.

As a new data practitioner, remember to look for that metadata; if it isn't available, ask for it. If you can't get it at all, be wary of how accurate the data visualization is.

Sometimes, a simple table is better…not all data should be forced into pretty, colorful displays. The data displays should add value. What else can we say here – sometimes simple is just better. If you are being asked to develop a data visualization that doesn't seem to make sense, or that doesn't help to tell the story in a way that makes it easier for people to understand, then stick to the simple data table that tells the simple story that your audience will understand.

Data visualizations should conform with basic data display principles, like those expressed by Edward Tufte: They should show the data; shouldn't distort data, should be scaled properly, and shouldn't contain elements that don't add value (Tufte calls this "chart junk").[7] Remember that design elements should add value.

As a new data practitioner, remember to KISS the data – Keep It Simple Sweetie. Display the data in a straightforward and honest way.

Resist the temptation to add bells and whistles so that you look clever. You won't.

For example, a non-profit organization might be tempted to embed ghosted images of clients, or scenes, in the background which may look sophisticated, but actually distract the reader from the important data being presented.

Some contend that "if you have to explain a data visualization it isn't very good." While data visualizations should be as intuitive as possible, sometimes there is value in using a data visualization even if it needs to be supported by explanation or facilitation. Complex displays, showing multiple variables or movement over time, may require some explanation to help the reader understand the complex nature of the subject. This does not make them bad – and they may be very powerful, in certain settings.

As a new data practitioner, realize there is a difference in what we are explaining here from the bells and whistles we write about above. Think about the explanation or facilitation like a teacher or a tour guide who helps the viewer to walk through a complex maze. A very complicated idea or situation can't always be explained with a simple display and no elaboration.

Remember that the concept of a dashboard is to signal that something needs checking. It is not a substitute for a more elaborate analysis that may include many other measures and

---

Data Savvy People

Data displays have their own language and the data person creating them can be so used to the language of the display that they don't realize it is often not obvious to others. When you are explaining a figure or data analysis result to people in other areas of your organization or clients, never assume that they know the visual language you are using. This language includes not just terms, but the actual elements of visualization that you take for granted as a data professional (e.g., what each mark on the graph represents; what measure each axis is showing; which axis you are talking about).

1. Don't just show the display and state the conclusion – first, explain the display elements to your audience so that they can understand *for themselves* what it is about your display that supports the claim. After all, maybe you have made a mistake that they can catch!

2. Your colleagues and customers often have knowledge that you don't have about the underlying process or phenomenon – but unless you take the time to make sure they can interpret the display FOR THEMSELVES, you probably won't find out those insights.

3. Do not assume people will proactively ask questions when they don't understand – especially when there are organizational power differentials in the room.

4. You need to explain the visual language and then give a little time and space for them to "get it."

Source: Thanks to Meg Streams, PhD,[8] for development of this callout

---

comparisons. When the engine light in your car's dashboard lights up, it doesn't signal exactly what is wrong. It tells you that something needs to be checked. In the same way, a data dashboard might show that an important outcome measure is not where we would like it to be, but may not, by itself, help us understand why it is not where we would like.

Conversely, data dashboards should encourage critical comparisons... guide the viewer to make appropriate comparisons, and prevent the viewer from making inappropriate ones.

Example 1: Small Multiples

Edward Tufte, like Galileo before him, advocates for the use of small multiples...repeated use of the same display to facilitate comparison. In this example, the same map of Hartford Neighborhoods is used to support comparisons of the services provided to participants by neighborhood, by type of service. Notice how the multiples make it easy to do the comparison...an example of the comparison being "embedded" in the data display (Figure 7.9).

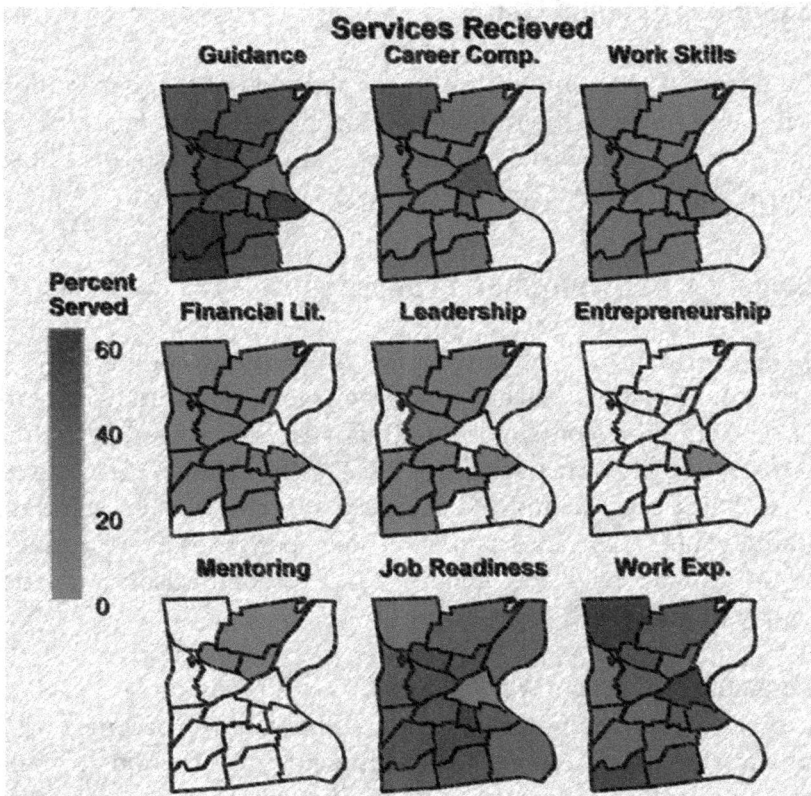

FIGURE 7.9 Small multiples example. *Source:* Created by the authors.

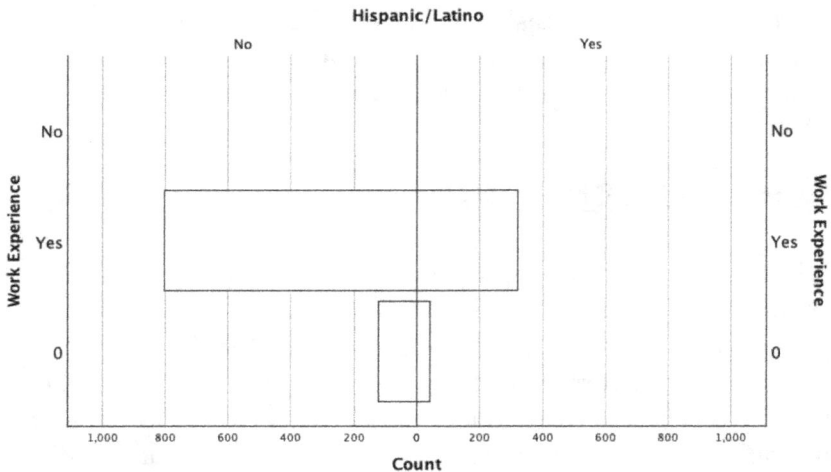

FIGURE 7.10 Pyramid chart example. *Source:* Created by the authors.

Example 2: Pyramid Chart

The pyramid chart allows for the comparison of the distribution of the difference in the number of youth receiving work experience program for those who are Hispanic or Latino and those who are not (Figure 7.10).

Example 3: High Information Density Display

This performance dashboard allows for multiple comparisons... between measures, over time, between measurement categories, and between snapshots (this year/prior year). While it seems extremely dense (and it is), users are able to orient themselves fairly quickly and the standard format helps soothe data qualms. This is also an example of how sparklines (miniaturized trendlines) can help add another kind of comparison and add interest (Figure 7.11).

Infographics—"Danger Will Robinson!"

A note about infographics. Infographics have become very popular, for good reason. They can send unambiguous signals regarding very specific data findings. They give just the highlights

Juvenile Justice System----- Population or System Performance Metric Dashboard	Most Recent Available Year	One Year Prior	Five Year Trend
	2017	2016	
Total Unique Clients Served	8485	10567	
Youth Justice Involvement Rate	2.14%	2.67%	
12 Month Recidivism Rate For All Those Referred To Court	2016	2015	
New Arrests	44.0%	43.0%	
Adjudication/Conviction	19.0%	18.9%	
	2016	2015	
Juvenile Detentions	1080	1261	
Committed Delinquent to CITS	140	207	
Committed Delinquent to Congregate Care	164	224	
Committed Delinquent to Detention/Corrections	148	146	
Committed Delinquent to Parole	215	288	
	2016	2015	
12 Month Recidivism Rate For All Those Under Supervision	46.0%	42.8%	
Outcomes for Children Refered to Court	2017	2016	
Convicted (Probation)	1372	1358	
Convicted (Discharged)	859	749	
Convicted (DCF Commitment)	275	257	
Transfer to Adult Court	152	180	
Non Judicial Supervision	2591	2207	
Not Guilty or Dismissed	5826	5115	
CT Four Year Graduation Rate	2016-2017	2015-2016	
Statewide	87.9%	87.4%	
Eligible For Free Lunch	76.0%	74.4%	
CT Chronic Absenteeism Rate	2017-2018	2016-2017	
Statewide	10.7%	9.9%	
Eligible for Free Lunch	18.8%	18.3%	
School Suspensions	2016-2017	2015-2016	
in school	53057	56866	
out of school	32982	34415	
	2016-2017	2015-2016	
School-Based Court Referrals	1626	1630	
	2017	2015	
Health Index	18.6	19.3	
mental/behavioral risks	13.5	14.6	
safety	12.6	11.8	
nutrition	19.8	23.3	
fitness	25.4	25.8	
substance abuse	21.5	18.1	

FIGURE 7.11 High information data display example. *Source:* Created by the authors.

of much more elaborate and complex analyses in easily digestible form. This is no doubt useful and can be important in fostering data democracy. But – you knew there was a but, didn't you? – the same thing that makes infographics easy to understand and powerful, is something that can be abused. Infographics are by their very nature SELECTIVE about what data are shown and not shown. This very practice is one area where statisticians and other data promulgators have earned a bad name. Infographics tend to ignore or minimize data that might not be consistent with the primary findings being shared, and it is usually not desirable to create infographics with lots of caveats. Infographics tend to suggest the world is less complex than it is, and therefore should be viewed with caution. We do not contend that infographics or the infographic approach are never appropriate or useful, but we do think great care must be taken not to fall into the data selectivity without transparency trap.

Data Storytelling: Sometimes There Is Not a Story to Tell—Yet

There are a lot of good resources out there that provide excellent guidance on developing and telling data stories. We highly recommend the book, *Storytelling with Data* by Cole Nussbaumer Knaflic.[9] We offer a couple of additional thoughts on this topic. First, we want to applaud the new emphasis on telling good data stories. This is one remedy to the "let's spit out and display a thousand tables and charts and call it analysis" problem. However, we do want to note that sometimes there is not a story to tell, yet. When you are first collecting data on a program, or a social problem, or almost anything, it may be a while before you have enough good data to tell a story. It may be appropriate, in those instances, to make the lack of data the story and advocate for further data development. Other times, the story is ambiguous, and few of us are good at telling ambiguous stories where we have to say, "it could suggest this, but it could also be that, but maybe it is something else." Doesn't sound like much of a story, does it? The caution here is to not let our need to tell a succinct and compelling data story lead us to OVER INTERPRET the data we have, or lead us to again fall into the data selectivity without transparency trap.

This is not to say we shouldn't keep trying to develop good data stories. When done well, without over-interpretation or selectivity without transparency, a good data story, supported by appropriately calibrated data displays, can be a very useful and powerful tool. And we will be the first to admit that some selectivity – directing the reader/audience to specific data points or trends – is necessary and appropriate. Just be intentional – and transparent – in your choices when you create your storyboard and get ready to tell your data story.

Notes

1 *Cambridge Dictionary of Philosophy*, 2nd ed., 1999, ed. Robert Audi.
2 *A Kant Dictionary*, 1995, by Howard Caygill.
3 The data used in the following examples are simulated in order to make the different approaches we are discussing apparent and readily understandable.
4 https://chartio.com/learn/charts/what-is-a-scatter-plot/#:~:text= A%20scatter%20plot%20(aka%20scatter,to%20observe%20 relationships%20between%20variables.
5 Roger Ariew, *Ockham's Razor: A Historical and Philosophical Analysis of Ockham's Principle of Parsimony*, 1976.
6 Simon, Herbert, *Administrative Behavior: A Study of Decision-Making Processes in Administrative Organization*. New York: Macmillan, 1947.
7 Tufte, Edward R., *The Visual Display of Quantitative Information*, Cheshire: Graphics Press, 1983.
8 CALLOUT developed by Meg Streams, PhD, Tennessee State University.
9 Knaflic, Cole Nussbaumer, *Storytelling with Data*, Hoboken, NJ: Wiley&Sons, 2015.

8

Approaches to Reducing Fears Related to Use

Earlier in this book, we discussed the two main types of data fear, and we have focused much of our discussions on fear related to a lack of skill. Fear related to use, and how others could misinterpret or misuse one's data after it has been shared or published, requires a different kind of approach. The following are several basic tools that can be used to mitigate fears related to the use of data.

Performing a Risk Assessment and Mitigation Plan

As Ron discussed in his Anxiety Buster, fears related to how data are used require a risk assessment and mitigation plan. This includes an understanding and articulation of the specific risks to be mitigated, as well as one or more associated mitigation strategies. To the extent possible, a plan for implementing these solutions should also be developed.

There are three additional strategies, in particular, that have almost universal application that should be part of an analyst, manager, or executive leader's toolkit along with the risk assessment and mitigation plan:

DOI: 10.4324/9781003496328-12

Anticipatory Interpretation

An essential strategy to address the risks associated with worries that data will be mischaracterized or misinterpreted is to offer anticipatory interpretation. One can usually guess in what ways the information being reported will be misinterpreted. If those are known, the data promulgator can offer their own interpretation together with the data, countering specific anticipated "pain points" and characterizing the data in a way that reduces the risk of the weaponization of the data. Taking the following steps makes it more difficult for the reader to actually misinterpret or misunderstand the data:

1. Review the data, or report, identifying those potential "pain points."
2. Specifically describe:
   a) where misunderstandings are likely to occur.
   b) how the data should be understood.
   c) potential misinterpretations – and why those misinterpretations are incorrect.

Preemptive Solution Identification

Even when clear data interpretations are offered, program performance or other problems may be revealed to stakeholders or the public in a highly visible way. One way of mitigating risks associated with "visible problems" in the data, such as having those data weaponized against the organization, is to preemptively offer solutions to those problems. That way, the organization is not just reporting data that reveal problems and shrugging their shoulders…they are seen as actively seeking and identifying potential solutions to those problems. It is even better to be able to report that a particular solution (or solutions) is already being piloted or otherwise implemented. Two ways of doing this are contextualizing the data, and identifying the problem, and how it will be addressed.

Contextualizing the data means explaining the factors that contribute to the condition reflected in the data so that the reader understands why a situation exists, or why a problem may have occurred. One example of that could be a job training program being delivered early in the pandemic. No matter how well the program did at pivoting services to an online delivery format, training participants, and assisting participants in developing job-related skills, for a significant period of time, businesses were not hiring. That is an important fact that, when shared, could help readers understand the low levels of job placements for a particular period of time.

Identifying the problem and the proposed solution goes one step further than just contextualizing the data. Contextualizing the data explains why the data are what they are, and how to understand them. Sometimes a solution may not yet be evident; but when the solution can be identified and shared, it can serve two useful purposes related to misinterpretation and mischaracterization: the first useful purpose is to acknowledge there is a problem, which demonstrates that you are not trying to hide or explain-away the problem; AND that a solution has been identified so that mischaracterization and misuse of the data are less likely; the second useful purpose is controlling your story by telling the story yourself, and telling it before anyone else has the opportunity to misunderstand, mischaracterize, or misuse your data – potentially changing how further audiences may understand the story and judge – or misjudge – the program.

Using Transparency as an Advantage

Finally, we have seen that when organizations are transparent and willingly share key data with funders and other stakeholders, like legislators, interest groups, or other executive leaders, the organizations are generally looked upon favorably. This is particularly true when other organizations are doing the opposite… reporting little or no data, being very selective about the data they report, or doing mental gymnastics to excessively "spin" the data to "explain away" performance problems.

We were present when a state agency presented a report to a legislative committee that demonstrated poor program performance. The presenters were upfront and clear about the goals that weren't met, and the fact that due to not meeting those goals, the program did not earn all the funding it needed to operate fully. When asked for the reason for poor performance, the presenters shared that they had not been funded for a key staff position; further, they were able to demonstrate the potential increase in program income if that position were to be funded. They left the hearing with a promise of the additional funding they needed to perform well. By honestly sharing negative performance data, the reason for the poor performance, how it had further impacted the program (loss of income), and how the problem could be mitigated, the presenters earned the trust and confidence of the legislative committee members, and left the hearing with the best possible outcome – a promise to make the program whole so that it could improve performance in the upcoming year.

Being transparent, reporting data comprehensively and honestly, and offering viable solutions to any performance issues raised can truly be an advantage when advocating for a program or requesting sustained or additional funding. The goodwill this generates is only amplified when the organization **follows up** in the next reporting period, showing how performance has changed since implementing any proposed solutions.

Fear of Skill Combined with Fear of Use

Fear of skill combined with fear of use is a particularly insidious combination. Often, it boils down to a lack of confidence in the data you produce, combined with a fear of that data being misinterpreted and used against your organization, and also incorporating the fear of not having the skill to combat, or stop, the misuse.

Remember, change happens in baby steps, and you may continue to experience some level of fear as you start to work more with data. Using your own Anxiety Buster, and any of the other tools in the toolbox, you can continue to address your fear(s) related to your skills. By performing a risk assessment and mitigation plan, as described in Ron's Anxiety Buster, and utilizing one or more of the three strategies described in this section, you can continue to address the fears related to use. And don't forget to call on your data mentor for some guidance, or when you feel the need for some reinforcement or a review of your work.

Data Meditation: Appropriate Responsibility

One great source of fear regarding performance data is related to fear of being measured on factors that are not in an organization's control. Of course, every program is affected by factors outside of the control of the program, like cultural factors, economic factors, and environmental factors. Sometimes, however, there can be an essential confusion between measuring the **impact** of a program at the community level and the **outcomes** generated for those receiving program services. Mark Friedman calls this distinction the difference between **population accountability** and **performance accountability**.[1] At the population level, we measure the extent to which we are achieving a particular quality of life result for the whole population, whereas at the performance level, we measure the extent to which we are achieving expected outcomes for those directly served by the program.

Confusion can occur when attempts are made to hold a program accountable using population-level measures. For example, a small anti-gun violence street program might be examined by looking at the number of shooting incidents in the community or the homicide rate. This is not an appropriate assignment of responsibility to the program. A small anti-gun violence program, *by itself*, is not likely to significantly affect the overall number of shooting incidents or the homicide rate. An appropriate assignment of responsibility to that program would be related to the individuals served by that program – perhaps a reduction in gun charges, or a reduction in other kinds of criminal activities, for those individuals. If the number of shooting incidents or homicide rate does increase, it does not necessarily mean that the anti-gun violence street program is ineffective *for those that they served*. In the same way, if the number of shooting incidents or homicide rate decreases, it is unlikely that the small street violence program was the sole cause of the decrease. There may have been other factors—other programs, other external factors, that also contributed to the decrease. As Mark Friedman notes, the most that can be said is that the small anti-gun violence street program *contributed* to the decrease in shooting incidents or homicide rate.[2]

Consider the following programs. What kind of measures would relate to the community or population level, and what kind might be related to client outcomes for the program? The first two lines are examples:

Program	Community/Population Measure	Program Outcome Measure
Anti-Gun Violence Program	Homicide Rate	Percent of individuals served who have no further justice involvement
Substance Abuse Program	Overdose Death Rate	Percent of individuals served who are clean 6 months after completing the program
Apprenticeship Program		
Low Income Housing Program		
Air Pollution Mitigation Program		
Community Economic Development Program		
Alternative Education Program for Youth at Risk of Disengagement		

Hopefully, you were able to think of some community-level, or population-level, measures for the middle column – measures that would show changes for a whole population of people, including those who didn't participate in any programs. Those measures might include things like overall air quality, higher graduation rates, higher employment rates, and a reduction in the rates of homelessness. If you were able to think of some program-related measures, depending on the program, those might have included program graduates who were hired, or who stayed in school, who found housing or started businesses, and program participants with fewer asthma symptoms or fewer visits to the emergency room.

Understanding the right level of accountability for a program versus a community-level project helps to clarify the level and types of data that should be collected, analyzed, and reported at both the program and the community levels. Equally important, correctly aligning the data to the program or project, helps the reader to focus on the right things: like what kind of outcomes can be anticipated for a small program versus a large community project. Providing clarity for the reader makes it more difficult for the reader to misinterpret or misuse the data.

Notes

1 Trying Hard Is Not Good Enough.
2 Trying Hard Is Not Good Enough.

Part IV

Moving Beyond Individual Data Fear

9

Organizational Data Fear

Data fear not only affects individuals. It can also infect teams, organizations, partnerships, collaboratives, and decentralized networks of services. We will refer to these types of data fears as organizational data fears. In group settings, data fear can prevent us from collectively developing effective strategies, planning processes, and services and from participating in continuous improvement and problem-solving. It can be a barrier to understanding "what works" and demonstrating the value and success of our collective efforts.

Organizational data fear is rooted in individual data fear and can manifest itself differently at the organizational level in that individual fear feelings and behaviors are reinforced by the like-minded data-fearing and data-avoiding behaviors of colleagues. This can result in groupthink, a phenomenon first described by the psychologist Irving Janis in 1972.[1] Janis described group behavior where otherwise rational individuals, in an attempt to preserve consensus, fail to examine alternatives, risks, or contrary data to a solution that is being proposed or implemented.[2] This can negatively impact organizations and groups in multiple ways.

Data fear can be contagious; if it becomes pervasive, it can create a persistent "anti-data" cultural norm. When regular use of data is avoided, organizations can miss important signals regarding how well their processes and programs are working, and whether expected outcomes are being achieved. Without

DOI: 10.4324/9781003496328-14

those signals, organizations often resort to "management by gut." "Management by gut" can be described as using your "gut", or intuition, to make management decisions. This can include interpreting processes that run smoothly and have no complaints, or viewing providers that accept all referrals and are pleasant to deal with, as successful – even if there is no evidence to back up that interpretation of success. Sometimes this thinking is informed by anecdotal information, or stories, instead of data, which we call "management by anecdote."

"Management by anecdote" is another trap that organizations can fall into by generalizing individual success stories as indicative of the overall success of a program or initiative. Some organizations that are not very comfortable using data tell stories about successful clients or programs instead. These stories then become the basis for managerial decisions, which can be very dangerous because by definition such an approach does not provide a comprehensive picture of performance. In moving to a data-informed approach, it should be pointed out to staff that one story by itself is just a story; but when stories are systematically gathered and aggregated, they become useful qualitative data.

"Management by gut" and "management by anecdote" can also include a very honest effort to address the things we feel need to be fixed by doing the things we feel are the right things. However, often there is no evidence that the things we feel are the "right things" actually work or what possible negative consequences there might be to implementing managerial intuition. In addition to leading organizations to erroneous conclusions, they can send negative signals to funders. When organizations rely on intuition and stories and hesitate to share data, funders and oversight agencies can become suspicious, lose confidence, or feel the organization has something to hide.

It may seem counterintuitive, but many organizations that operate with a data fear or data avoidance culture actually collect significant amounts of data. This might include data required by funders, data that are no longer required by funders but are still being collected, or data that may be collected for good reason, but just isn't being used. In our work, we have heard from many contracted providers over the years who are frustrated by the time it takes them to collect and submit data to funding agencies, and never hear back about those reports – were they accurate? Were they useful? Did they indicate good – or poor – performance? Were they ever read?

In short, these organizations have data but don't use data. They may be collecting data they don't need, and missing out on data that could be useful. They are doing the work of collecting, reporting, and storing information about their efforts without reaping the benefits of learning from the data they have collected. Moving away from a fear culture and toward a data-embracing culture is hard, but it is possible.

Attempting to understand and utilize data, to diagnose problems and to identify the best remedies or solutions, is a different way of approaching the work. Such efforts can be challenging because they include addressing organizational culture. However, investing the time and energy to learn and apply data-informed approaches is well worth the extra work. We will identify some steps organizations can take to change the culture. The first step is understanding an organization's culture relative to comfort or fear using data.

Organizational data fear should be addressed at both the individual and organizational levels. In organizations where data fear has been institutionalized as a cultural norm, the standard operating procedure is often to share as little data as possible, keep data "close to the vest," and include as little data as possible in reports. This is often accompanied by an overtly hostile attitude toward data – "we don't have time for that stuff here—we are helping people." When new people enter the organization, they are quickly indoctrinated into the "anti-data" cultural norm and can actually begin to regress as far as their data comfort is concerned, so it is important to put lots of support into place when addressing a data fear culture. Multiple types of support need to be provided based on the type of organization, current organizational data comfort and capacity, needs, staff roles, and different learning styles. Support can include:

◆ identifying early data users and early adopters of data-driven decision-making, and they and other colleagues in the organization who are further along on the data comfort continuum should be encouraged to be mentors and support their more anxious peers

◆ Leadership training/visioning/planning to utilize data in ongoing management decision-making, planning, and performance management/continuous quality improvement

◆ Establishing practical and realistic performance measures and related reports

◆ Staff appropriately: adequately trained and competent staff; staff who believe in the effort, enough time, and resources to devote to managing data/reporting/performance

◆ Training that includes ongoing support

◆ Data coaching: in-house; nonprofits; universities

Assessing Data Fear at the Organizational Level

When assessing data fear at the organizational level, reviewing the different levels of data fear and data comfort in the chart below, and the related explanations, will help with understanding how many organizations approach using data based on levels of data fear or data comfort. The organizational data fear assessment (see Appendix B) provides an opportunity to determine the extent to which an organization or collaborative fits one of these levels of data fear or data comfort (Table 9.1).

Data-fearing organizations will avoid using data or performing data tasks to plan and report the organization's efforts, effectiveness, successes, and areas where improvements can be made. Staff members may push back on pressure to use data, stating that data are overrated, there is no time to create and use data reports, and that their focus is on serving clients or constituents.

Data-avoiding organizations will also avoid using data and offer many of the same reasons. However, there may be

TABLE 9.1 Organizational Data Fear-Comfort Continuum

Organizational Data Comfort Level	Organizational Data Culture	Organizational Behaviors Related to Data Capacity	Organizational Behaviors Related to Data Use	Organizational Developmental Task	Fear-Fighting Approach
Data-Fearing Organization	**Avoidance**	Staff in my organization identify as "non-data" people	Staff in my organization avoid or defer data tasks	Introduce the importance of using data to make decisions and understand performance	Basic Training; Address individual data fear; provide support through data mentors
Data-Avoiding Organization	Avoidance	Most staff in my organization believe or contend that "data don't matter" but there are a few "data visionaries"	My organization shares as little data as possible	Establish use of data reports with review and support sessions	Basic and ongoing Training; Address individual data fear; provide support through data mentors
Data Developing Organization	Crossover / threshold	Staff in my organization sometimes use data to understand how we are doing.	My organization sometimes uses data to make decisions, and sometimes reviews and uses performance data for	Establish practice of creating, submitting, and using data reports on a regular basis, including discussing with	Ongoing training; support through data mentors; establish in-house data champion network; provide safe opportunities

(Continued)

TABLE 9.1 (*Continued*)

Organizational Data Comfort Level	Organizational Data Culture	Organizational Behaviors Related to Data Capacity	Organizational Behaviors Related to Data Use	Organizational Developmental Task	Fear-Fighting Approach
		Management sometimes includes staff members in discussions about performance, and is starting to use data reports to understand performance	improvement; is starting to use charts, infographics, and other data visualizations in presentations and reports	staff members, to understand performance and inform decisions	for new data practitioners to create and use data that impacts their work
Data-Using organization	Comfort	Staff in my organization use data regularly to understand how we are doing	There is a general recognition that data are important and have value	Further Reinforce practice of creating, submitting, and using data reports on a regular basis, to understand performance and inform	Ongoing training; support through data mentors; support in-house data champion network; provide safe

(*Continued*)

TABLE 9.1 (Continued)

Organizational Data Comfort Level	Organizational Culture	Organizational Behaviors Related to Data Capacity	Organizational Behaviors Related to Data Use	Organizational Developmental Task	Fear-Fighting Approach
				decisions, across all organizational units Develop ways to celebrate and support use of data within and across the organization	opportunities for new data practitioners to create and use data that impacts their work
Data-Embracing Organizations	Comfort	Staff in my organization use data regularly to understand how we are doing	My organization regularly reviews performance data and uses these data for continuous improvement	Further Reinforce practice of creating, submitting, and using data reports on a regular basis, to understand performance and inform decisions, across	Ongoing training; support through data mentors; support in-house data champion network; provide safe opportunities

(Continued)

TABLE 9.1 (*Continued*)

Organizational Data Comfort Level	Organizational Data Culture	Organizational Behaviors Related to Data Capacity	Organizational Behaviors Related to Data Use	Organizational Developmental Task	Fear-Fighting Approach
				all organizational units, and enhance accountability with regular public facing reports Enhance ways to celebrate and support use of data within and across the organization	for new data practitioners to create and use data that impacts their work; provide guidance and mentorship to other organizations

Source: Created by the authors.

pockets of data users in specific units or divisions, and there may be a small group of data visionaries within the organization who try to promote the use of data in the organization. Organizational leaders do not support the promotion of data use in the organization.

Data-developing organizations realize the need for data and start using data on a regular basis, but are not yet comfortable doing so, and don't yet use data consistently. Developmental tasks for this level of organization include supporting and reinforcing the use of data in reports and decision-making efforts on a regular and consistent basis and finding ways to support and celebrate staff use of data in reporting and decision-making.

Data-using organizations have found a level of comfort in using data and have begun to use data on a regular basis to understand performance. It is important for these organizations to continue providing support and training, and to encourage efforts to utilize data to understand and improve performance.

Data-embracing organizations regularly use and support the use of data across the organization. In addition to using data to understand performance, these organizations also utilize data in continuous improvement efforts and share data-based reports freely inside and outside of the organization. These organizations are in a position to assist other organizations on their data use journeys and may be able to provide support, mentorship, and even training to other organizations.

You can see how our prior discussions regarding the nature of individual data fear can be similar to the ways in which organizations do or do not behave, as demonstrated in the chart above. Remember – organizations are made up of people, each of whom has their own level of data fear or comfort, and over time, organizations can evolve a collective cultural bias against, or for, the use of data. All of the tools we have shared that can help individuals address data fear can also help at the organizational level.

However, other actions may be necessary to catalyze, incent, encourage, and support individual efforts to transcend data fear in an organizational setting.

Creating and Supporting a Data-Informed Organizational Culture

The message that an organization should become data-informed and embrace the use of data should come from the top. When organizational leaders send the message that data are important, and their use is expected, it sends a strong message to staff members at all levels of the organization and can be very helpful in both starting and sustaining the necessary culture change. If the message doesn't come from the very top of the organization, it can still be meaningful; in cases where the message comes from someone other than the agency's leader, it is important that leadership supports the effort and, at a minimum, does not interfere with efforts to actively share or use data made by different teams or divisions of the organization.

A data-informed culture takes work to create and support. Organizational efforts to create data-informed cultures do not occur in a vacuum and must be able to incorporate ongoing operations and projects and support staff members who may suffer from data fear.

In the same way that individuals can experience the crossover effect of both types of data fear, organizations can also experience the same crossover effect. That can include when organization staff are uncomfortable creating and using data for reporting and management purposes and are then doubly fearful based on their concerns that other individuals or organizations may misinterpret or misuse the data, and they as the report creator(s) will not have the data-related skills to catch, clarify, or correct someone else's misinterpretation or misuse of the data.

Data Savvy People

Having team members who are new data professionals, and who have overcome, or are working to overcome, their data fear, can be a gift, because although they have worked to overcome their fears, they are still in touch with some of the ways that working with data can leave one open to risks. The way they approach the work may include their attention to detail (based on their concerns about their own skills); their awareness of fundamental misunderstandings that might be at play; and because they still relate to the anxiety about being too quick to act on or publicize data that point to problems, they are more likely to identify potential opportunities for offering solutions as a risk mitigation approach.

It is equally important to remember that the ongoing work of the organization does not stop while staff members, departmental teams, and leadership are working to become more comfortable with data and starting to move toward a data-informed culture.

We have found that "looking backwards" at current efforts in order to be able to retrofit a data structure can be very useful. The look backwards consists of asking and answering questions that consider and confirm why the program or effort was originally initiated; what the desired outcomes were; whether those desired outcomes are still relevant or if they have changed; what success looks like; how we would be able to recognize success; and what the necessary actions are (i.e., implementation of the program or effort) in order to achieve that success. The specific questions might look like the following:

Why did we fund this program?
What were we hoping to achieve?

What would success look like?
Do we have a way to measure that?
And how are we actually doing?[3]

Going through the "look backwards" exercise is valuable for multiple reasons. First, it is a great way to introduce teams of staff members to a data discussion in a non-threatening way and use familiar and accessible language. Second, it very directly supports the organization's efforts in creating a data-informed culture, and third, it empowers the participants to create the data structure for a specific initiative so that they understand the data and why the data matter.

Sometimes going through the "look backwards" exercise will reveal that based on the stated outcomes, the program or effort under consideration may not be consistent with the identified actions to achieve those outcomes – and the program or effort may require some redesigning. This topic has some overlap with developing useful performance measures, but for the moment, we will stay focused on creating data comfort and leave performance measure development for another discussion.

From an organizational perspective, helping individual staff members and departmental teams learn the importance of data, and supporting them in their use of data, strengthens the organization's data-informed culture. Empowering the organization's staff members to understand whether their work works in achieving desired outcomes strengthens not only the organization's data-informed culture, but also strengthens the effectiveness of the organization as it begins to use data.

Data Savvy People

Allow your colleagues to bring their "package of reality" to the analysis. Other people can see things that you can't – based on their unique lived experiences, their interactions with customers, and their personal approach to problem-solving, and when empowered, they will bring these important skills and attributes to the analysis table.

As data culture change is occurring, it is important to recognize and be okay with the fact that this may occur in "baby steps." Sometimes "anti-data" culture is deep-seated and has taken decades to develop; so, we should not expect an overnight transformation. With these baby steps will come baby successes – "little victories" that should be celebrated and made widely known. This will allow positive data energy to permeate and saturate the organization.

Finally, as organizations take baby steps in creating data-informed cultures, organizational leaders and staff members will experience the power of knowing their own data and being able to tell the story behind it – in other words, controlling their own story. When it is a positive story, celebrate it; when the story is one that identifies the need for improvement, it is equally important to tell one's own story, identify and share the issue that was found, and be able to identify and share how the organization will address the issue moving forward.

Notes

1 Janis, Irving L., *Victims of Group Think: A Psychological Study of Foreign Policy Decisions and Fiascos*. Boston, MA: Houghton-Mifflin, 1972.
2 https://www.psychologytoday.com/us/basics/groupthink.
3 Adapted from Mark Friedman's *Trying Hard Is Not Good Enough*, 2005.

10

Collaborative Data Fear

Just as individual data fear can infect an organization, organizational data fear can infect a partnership, collaborative, or decentralized network of service providers (we call these DSNs). A DSN is a formal or informal group of organizations that provide an array of services to achieve a related set of outcomes. DSNs can be collaboratives, but not all collaboratives are DSNs – especially those that do not emphasize service provision. Many collaboratives, and DSNs in particular, include multiple organizations with varying intergovernmental and/or intersectoral relationships. They often lack structured, hierarchical relationships and include third party service provision with multiple funding streams. Individual organizations within the network may provide different kinds of services, some overlapping. These organizations are often competitors as well as collaborators and network partners.

In either case, when multiple organizations contending with varying levels of data fear come together, any latent data fear can spread across organizations, and manifest itself in new ways related to sharing and integrating data, measuring outcomes, and reporting on individual and collective efforts.

How Data Fear Can Spread

Aside from all the ways data fear manifests itself in individuals and in organizations, data fear can also reveal itself in different

DOI: 10.4324/9781003496328-15

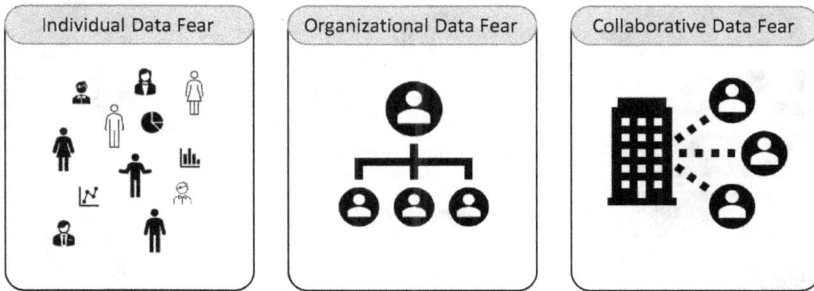

FIGURE 10.1 Spread of data fear.
Source: Created by the authors.

ways when collaboratives and DSNs are considered. There are many challenges related to the collection and use of data for such entities. There is often a lack of a formal accountability structure, with no clear way of mandating or standardizing common data collection or measurement approaches. Organization and provider data capacity may vary substantially. There are often multiple types of customers, participants, or target recipients of services, and not all expected outcomes apply to all service providers or service streams. These challenges would exist, even without the introduction of the complicating factor of data fear. Add another factor: getting organizations within a collaborative or DSN on the same page regarding the use of data can be like herding cats, and addressing these issues becomes an even greater challenge. Cats are temperamental and independent, as are many fear-laden organizations within a service network. You need to have special tools to be able to successfully herd finicky organizational partners (see Figure 10.2).

Creation of a Common Measurement Frame for Collaboratives and DSNs

One of the primary cat-herding challenges, and also one of the primary solutions to the multiple challenges, is the creation of a common measurement framework for collaboratives and DSNs. This has to start with the identification of shared goals– the overarching results that bring them together and which they are trying to achieve as a group. Things to consider in the goal

Catnip	Gain cooperation (what's in it for me) and buy-in
Clean Litter Box	Show it is ok to dispense with unnecessary measurement
Cat Bed	Establish own space
Cat Toys	Sustain engagement with participatory process
Travel Crate	Establish a safe space to move forward
Scratching Posts	Work out frustrations
Hair Ball Remedy	Conflict resolution through clear and transparent decision process
Cat Treats	Celebrating the little victories

FIGURE 10.2 Cat tools.
Source: Created by the authors.

identification process include the quality of life results that collaborative members are trying to achieve for their customers, and how partner organizations can identify how they will benefit from such efforts, and how the collective can also benefit and demonstrate its value. In this process, the most likely "nexus of accountability," or "data affinity group," will reveal itself. This "affinity group" of organizations should be explicitly identified and supplemented to ensure diverse and appropriate representation.

The identified affinity group, along with any collaborative leadership and technical assistance providers, can utilize the same approaches that we recommend for overcoming data fear in organizations, with a couple of important additions:

- ◆ Creating common agreements on results to be achieved is a critical first step
- ◆ An important next step is creating a shared menu of measures that can be aligned with the different organizations' reporting systems through a common data dictionary
- ◆ And creating measures at different levels of granularity that relate to programs, organizations, and the

collaborative, or system, allows for system-level and cross-program measurement

Once the shared goals and population-level results are identified, collaborative members should be individually and collectively encouraged to use data and measure performance. In doing so, a flexible approach should be utilized, incorporating theories of change, strategies, and evidence-based practices. A menu of measures, with common operationalizations can be created and used as appropriate by different providers and programs. It is critical that customers and the front-line staff who are actually doing the work participate in the measurement development process. System level, cross-program measurement should also be emphasized. At all levels, diversity, equity, and inclusion measures should be identified and reported (more on this in a bit). These important process and outcome measures can serve as the foundation for formal process and outcome evaluations. Remember, you can't compare outcomes (as in a random control trial or comparison group study) unless you collect the appropriate outcome measurement information.

Data Savvy People

Analysis isn't done in a vacuum - facilitation, project planning, budgeting - having a team approach makes it more likely that your colleagues will increase their data skills and be able to contribute their experiences and perspectives to the work, thereby making it more complete. Those other colleagues have value to contribute—but only if the "data pro" takes the time to get them conversant with the visual language in use. Just being in the room or on a team isn't enough.

Mechanisms for integrating data across organizations and providers should be developed. Usually, a single application system is not possible, so a federated approach should be utilized. A key to the success of a federated system is for participating organizations to understand how they can benefit from contributed data and to be assured that data are safe and confidentiality is protected.[1]

Of course, not all of this development effort is going to happen instantaneously. Data integration approaches need to be piloted with a few early adopters. Integrated data need validation by the organizations providing the source data, and all organizations providing data need to validate public facing collaborative reports. This instills TRUST, which is critical for any collaborative effort and also one important way to ease data fear.

Ultimately, Collaboratives and DSNs should use the results of routine measurement and periodic focused evaluation efforts to understand performance and improve service across their networks (lather, rinse, repeat) ☺. As we have mentioned throughout this book, ensuring that adequate technical assistance and support are ALWAYS available is crucial.

Acknowledge, and Be Transparent about, Issues Related to Diversity, Equity and Inclusion

All population indicators, system measures, and common program measures can be disaggregated by gender, race, ethnicity, age, etc. These disaggregations form the basis for different kinds of comparisons related to diversity, equity, and inclusion. It is also important to include focused questions on customer and staff surveys related to measures of inclusion, such as feeling heard, feeling like they are being treated fairly, and knowing they have a place at the decision-making table. It is critical that these disaggregations and comparisons are reported and discussed just as routinely as the other measurement data and that strategies related to increasing diversity, ensuring equity, and fostering inclusion are developed and implemented by collaboratives/ DSNs. These conversations have to happen at every level, from the "high level governance" of the collaborative/DSN and related funders to the executive leadership teams of individual partner organizations to program managers, front-line service delivery staff, and customers.

Note

1 https://www.ctdata.org/about-hdc.

11

Creating and Sustaining a Data-Informed Culture

We have just discussed the different dimensions of data fear in an organizational context. Transcending those fears is easier in organizations that have a data informed culture: one where leaders encourage and sponsor data work; where adequate resources are allocated to collecting, compiling, analyzing, reporting, and using data; and where there are opportunities to receive appropriate technical assistance as needed. Culture building is one way to combat fear, and combatting fear is one way to build a data-informed culture; they are iterative and mutually catalyzing (Figure 11.1).

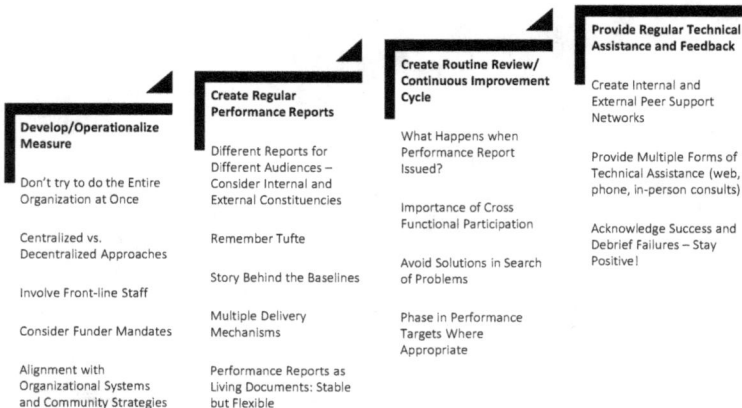

Develop/Operationalize Measure	Create Regular Performance Reports	Create Routine Review/ Continuous Improvement Cycle	Provide Regular Technical Assistance and Feedback
Don't try to do the Entire Organization at Once	Different Reports for Different Audiences – Consider Internal and External Constituencies	What Happens when Performance Report Issued?	Create Internal and External Peer Support Networks
Centralized vs. Decentralized Approaches	Remember Tufte	Importance of Cross Functional Participation	Provide Multiple Forms of Technical Assistance (web, phone, in-person consults)
Involve Front-line Staff	Story Behind the Baselines	Avoid Solutions in Search of Problems	Acknowledge Success and Debrief Failures – Stay Positive!
Consider Funder Mandates	Multiple Delivery Mechanisms	Phase in Performance Targets Where Appropriate	
Alignment with Organizational Systems and Community Strategies	Performance Reports as Living Documents: Stable but Flexible		

FIGURE 11.1 Above shows the basic elements of an approach to creating a data driven culture.

DOI: 10.4324/9781003496328-16

Developing and Operationalizing Measures

We don't have room in this book to go into all the technical details regarding the development and operationalization of performance measures and other data that you may routinely review in your organization. We recommend *Trying Hard Is Not Good Enough*[1] by Mark Friedman and *Performance Measurement: Getting Results*[2] by Harry Hatry for solid explications of the steps you need to take to develop performance measures. The point we stress here is that developing and using performance measures is important. Performance measures help the organization quantify and qualify what is important in the work; what the organization is striving to achieve; and how the organization is performing in relation to the identified measures.

Aside from these considerations, it is worth noting that the performance efforts should always be aligned with community, system, and organizational strategies so that they do not encourage actions that are inconsistent with other strategic efforts.

Beyond the actual technical processes used, there are a lot of considerations that you and your organization should be aware of if performance measures are being developed. If your organization is just starting to get into performance measurement, it is important not to take on too much right away. It is often better to start with one program, or one unit, as the focus of development efforts, and build on the success of early efforts. Baby steps! You can often find individual program managers and staff that will agree to be "early adopters" of the data-driven ethic; as this proliferates throughout the organization, these early adopters can, and do, form "data colonies" that share information, provide peer support, and leverage resources for professional development and technical assistance.

Provide Regular Technical Assistance and Feedback

As development efforts continue, it is also important to think through what technical assistance will be provided, and how it will be provided. We strongly recommend providing accessible, friendly, formal, and informal, technical assistance for all staff members. The technical assistance should be focused on three general areas: facilitating data use by helping data-anxious staff members feel more comfortable working with data; helping data-anxious staff improve their skills and ability to use data to create performance reports, including creating appropriate charts and graphs; helping data-anxious staff members to mitigate the risks their reports will contain inappropriate information (including privacy issues, or not conforming to legal requirements) or be misinterpreted, misused, or hijacked.

There is no one correct approach to how technical assistance should be delivered; some organizations favor the creation of a centralized data or performance unit, while others favor de-centralizing data analysis and performance measurement responsibility. We recommend a hybrid approach. We think it is important to have at least a small unit (or in very small organizations, one individual) who is responsible for creating a consistent approach to data collection, compilation, analysis, and reporting. This unit can often provide additional technical support to others in the organization who are embarking on data analytic activities. At the same time, it is desirable to encourage and empower individual program managers and staff to take up the data analytic gauntlet and participate in using data to manage their programs and make decisions. This decentralized aspect of performance measurement and data analysis is an important way to ensure that front line staff participate in data and performance measurement development, review of data and performance measures, and continuous improvement efforts.

Changing the culture at a data-fearing, data-avoiding organization is possible. It is important to remember that change takes time, and usually comes in baby steps. Celebrate the baby steps! They add up, and when you look back to where you started, you will see meaningful change!

Creating Performance Reports

The development and issuance of performance reports can certainly be a fear trigger, but there is much we can do to mitigate the potential triggering aspects of these activities. For example, providing the technical assistance referenced above; having clear, common sense performance measures; understanding that different groups will benefit from different levels of detail in reports; and also working with staff and program providers to both include their knowledge and experience to contextualize the reports, and help them understand what needs to be reported, and why it is important to report that information.

One important activity is to consider creating different reports for different audiences. Executives often need different measures and report elements than program managers. Program managers may need much more granular detail in their reports, with additional data that help to understand processes. Reports for external stakeholders are usually at a higher level of detail, with a greater emphasis on outcome measures. *Knowing that the reports being provided are properly "calibrated" for the intended audience can drastically reduce anxiety related to the issuance of reports.*

Another important aspect of report generation is ensuring that the data in the reports are shown in an accurate, comprehensive, and straightforward way. Tufte's data display principles are critically important here.[3] (See The Agonies and Ecstasies of Data Visualizations and Data Dashboards).

As we have emphasized elsewhere, the importance of adding context to the measures being reported cannot be understated. This is critical to building a data-informed culture because it helps to build trust – trust that measures are being fairly represented; trust that staff will be provided with an opportunity to empha-size important considerations; and trust that this allows for a genuine dialog regarding performance rather than measures triggering reflexive "gotchas."

Staff members who trust their story is being told fairly and accurately through data are more likely to use, learn from, and report data than if they don't trust how the data are being used. Staff members who trust they can go to a support person for help with report generation or analysis are more likely to push past their own comfort levels when working with data than if they fear their reports or analyses will be inaccurate or incorrect. And staff members who trust they can engage in a genuine performance dialogue within their organization are more likely to value, and benefit from, using data – whether creating reports, understanding reports, or utilizing reports to improve performance.

It is important to maintain the discipline of using proper reporting and data display principles, and including an effective story behind the baseline, even when using new reporting vehicles, like providing reports on a website or even pro-viding interactive data via a tool like Tableau. Recognize, too, that supporting narrative provided in reports is more likely to be ignored or marginalized when provided in some electronic format – so it is important to ensure that critical context does not get "left behind" in the process of delivering data electronically. When this happens, it can undermine the trust so important to building a data informed culture.

Organizations that are new to utilizing data to understand and improve performance may not need to start from scratch when creating and collecting data in order to understand performance. Often, the data are being reported, but not used. In our consulting, training, performance-system development, and program evalu-ation work, we often hear from program operators that they are required to submit reports to their funders on a regular basis, but never receive any response to, or questions about, those reports. Program operators state this lack of feedback feels to them like the data have disappeared into a black hole. Not surprisingly, this causes frustration on the part of the program operators; and is also a lost opportunity for both program operators and funders. (The converse can often be true too: funders often ask for information, and get no response from provider partners, thereby sending those requests and the potentially useful information into the same black hole as the unread reports.)

When embarking on an organizational effort to begin using data to understand performance, the first step should be to catalog and then leverage,data that are already collected instead of creating and generating a new set of reports. Once the existing data are being used, if additional data collection is necessary, connect the dots between the data collected and the ultimate use of the data. Staff members are often never told in detail why certain data are necessary; to ensure buy-in and accurate, timely data collection, help staff members understand why additional data collection is necessary, how the data will be used, and why it is important.

INCLUDE STAFF MEMBERS IN DATA DISCUSSIONS – not just as data consumers, but as valuable team members who may understand the story behind the data better than administrators, evaluators, or funders.

There are two more steps to consider as part of implementing or improving data collection and use efforts. The first is to avoid duplicating data entry whenever possible. If a set of data is being collected for one use and can be useful in a second effort, try to copy-and-save the data on an organizational level rather than having program staff re-report it. This may include collaboration with the agency's IT staff or consultants to automate the use of the same data for multiple purposes. The second step (which is almost guaranteed to increase the popularity level of whoever initiates this step) is to have staff members and program partners identify data elements that are being collected and reported, but aren't being used; and which they can stop reporting.

A final note related to data/performance reporting. It should be understood that, even when a lot of energy and resources have been expended to create report specifications, that reports should never be considered set in stone. While it is important for reports to be stable and include the same elements for comparison over time, when certain elements are no longer helpful, or require re-operationalization, that should happen. When new, and perhaps better, data become available, they should be added to the report. Flexibility and responsiveness in report development are critical to developing and maintaining trust.

Mitigating the Risks of Using, Sharing, and Reporting Data

Developing performance measures, creating regular performance reports, providing abundant and approachable technical assistance, creating a trusting environment, and communicating with, and involving staff members and providers in data collection and use, are all important factors in mitigating any potential risks that organizations could experience when sharing data and publishing reports. Let's discuss how creating good data and empowering staff and partners can increase accuracy, clarify intent, and help to ensure the data are not subject to misinterpretation or misuse.

Creating clear and appropriate performance measures and then utilizing the resulting data in performance reports focuses reporting efforts on the data and measures that matter most, and on which the organization should be focused; these measures should be aligned with the organization's ongoing work and become part of the organizational culture. With support and technical assistance, understanding, reporting, and using these measures to inform becomes part of everyone's work, and not an anxiety-provoking additional task for some members of the organization.

As part of the regular performance reporting, focusing on the performance measures, and contextualizing the data to tell the whole story and identify forces and circumstances that have helped or hindered the work

- ◆ Empower staff members and providers closest to the work to participate in reporting and analysis
- ◆ Pre-emptive strike by identifying your own interpretation of the measures/the data represented and also the solutions you are considering/getting ready to implement

◆ Identifying and acknowledging less than desirable performance, and creating and committing to routing performance review and performance management, as discussed below

◆ Ensuring privacy issues are understood and guidelines followed; and ensuring legal requirements for reporting are understood and adhered to.

Creating a Routine Review/Ongoing Performance Management/Continuous Improvement Cycle

A great deal of energy goes into data development, the selection and identification of performance measures, data collection, data analysis, and reporting. But if the reports are not utilized… if they do not actually inform decision-making, or catalyze continuous improvement efforts, then they are of severely limited utility. Thus, creating a process for routine, periodic review of data reports, and a process for using those reports for performance management and continuous improvement is a critical aspect of the development of a data-informed culture.

There has been a lot written around using data to inform decision making[4–7], and our intent is not to replicate those discussions here. However, there are a few key considerations that are worth mentioning, particularly in relation to reducing data fear and anxiety:

1. *Create a mutually understood expectation as to what happens when a performance report is issued*. The expectation should be that something happens…some process is triggered… rather than "oh…here is another report…there it goes into the pile…."

2. *Emphasize the cross-functional review of data*. When data are reviewed, the data review should include participants from different parts of the organization, including, possibly, and representation from fiscal/business management, human resources, legal, and strategy offices.

This provides different perspectives and helps to ensure important considerations are not missed or ignored. Also, the "non-data people" on the team can often use their enlightened ignorance to ask questions, or identify unarticulated assumptions, that get missed by more overtly data-oriented people. Most importantly, frontline staff should be included in these reviews, because they always have a better understanding of processes than others not actively participating in them. Frontline staff participation is also important because it helps to build trust that the performance process is not being "done" to them…instead, they are helping to improve processes and strengthen their organization.

3. Another way to build trust is to *avoid solutions in search of problems*[8]. It is often very obvious when suddenly performance problems are "noticed," and there is a ready solution at hand…a new process approach, a training program, some information technology application…that there was some agenda at some level of the organization to implement that solution…even if there wasn't necessarily an associated problem! A less egregious version of this is identifying a solution to a problem before the problem has been fully diagnosed. Rushing to a particular solution narrows the diagnostic effort and quickly eliminates other, potentially more appropriate solutions. We have been emphasizing trust in these culture-building efforts…trust that problems will be diagnosed fully and honestly, and that the solutions selected are not pre-ordained is one of the most important kinds of trust to build in this work.

4. *The creation of performance targets is another area where caution is required.* Trust will not be built if it is felt that performance targets are set in an arbitrary, heavy-handed, or unrealistic manner. The creation of an appropriate performance target starts with selecting the right measures for targets…setting targets for some kinds of measures, such as lagging outcome measures, may not be appropriate. Targets should not

be set until there is an adequate baseline for the measure to inform the setting of the target. Finally, targets should be realistic and achievable. While challenging staff is important, setting targets that are too high (or too low) will actually serve to demotivate staff. Finally, if performance targets are new to an organization, they should be phased in over time. Start by simply reporting the measure. Once sufficient baseline information is available, create a provisional target...simply showing staff what the target would be...before setting actual targets. What you do when a target is missed is also important. Avoid immediate punitive action. It should be considered a continuous improvement opportunity. Consider a progressive approach if performance continues to be below the target. All of these considerations also apply to setting targets in a performance contracting setting with third party service providers.

Sustaining A Data-Driven Culture

Once an organization has begun moving toward a data-driven culture following the approaches described above, there may come a time when that progress is threatened by a change in administration, changes in funder policies, or other programmatic changes. In these circumstances, it can be hard to maintain momentum and not lose the progress that has been made. While this can be challenging, there are a few essential building-blocks to sustain a data-driven culture in the face of such changes, including:

- ◆ Demonstrate Value
- ◆ Permeate and Saturate
- ◆ Use Stealth
- ◆ Be Flexible and Adaptive
- ◆ Integrate New Approaches

Demonstrate Value

You should always allow people to ask, "what's in it for me?" and "how does that fit with my goals and priorities?" And be able to answer. Being able to answer includes anticipating those two questions, and having some potential answers ready. This is especially true of new administrators or others who might be thinking that they need to reallocate resources or otherwise revamp current performance efforts. New leaders should be briefed on the work that has been done – don't be afraid to advocate for the continued emphasis on data! You should create a treasure chest of positive results of data-driven efforts. You should always be ready to share these success stories, and don't be shy about it! It is difficult to argue with better outcomes, cost savings, or improved efficiency!

Permeate and Saturate

What do we mean by this? To *saturate* means to "fill something so that it can hold no more, while *permeate* means to pass or trickle through another material. Both methods are important to sustain a data-driven culture in the face of change. For a garden to grow and flourish, you need to really saturate it so the water permeates the soil and gets down the roots. Similarly, you must saturate your agency with ongoing visible and accessible technical assistance, including follow-up. This must include line staff, management, and external stakeholders, and be helpful, non-threatening, empowering, consistent, and ongoing. Planting these data seeds throughout your organization will eventually result in the formation of affinity groups of data users, or "data colonies."

While having a "data unit" or "performance unit" is a good thing, allowing for the development of real technical expertise and support, this isn't enough; during times of transition or change these can easily be undermined, dissolved, or merged into units with other responsibilities that detract from the data work. This is when data colonies become so important...the data work is carried on despite possible lack of any central champion or mandate because it has become an important part of the work – not an add-on that can be eliminated

Another aspect of permeation and saturation has to do with the formation of external constituencies for the data produced by your organization. External stakeholders can maintain pressure for data and data work even when people inside the organization are reluctant, for various reasons, to continue to advocate for such data work. These external stakeholders can include funders, consumers, advocates, and advisory boards – all of whom have a vested interest in the success of the work and will rely on data and reports to understand progress towards success.

Use Stealth

Given our focus on transparency, it may seem ironic that we advocate for using stealth in this context. Sometimes it is better to do things quietly and persistently, supporting the permeation and saturation of data-driven thinking and approaches, rather than making a big deal of adopting these methods and then letting them slowly fade away – this is what we mean by "using stealth". Such constituency building, within and outside the organization, can be done one project at a time…or one data product at a time. It is the persistent application of the data-driven approaches we have discussed that is more important, than any one-time event or initiative. Avoid too much fanfare; avoid creating the "big splash with little follow-up" that can doom data initiatives, making them feel like the "flavor of the month." It's not the big kickoff party that matters; it is the consistent, everyday application of principles, approaches, and methodologies that matter.

Be Flexible and Adaptive

Part of sustaining a data-driven culture is maintaining consistency of approach and product; this builds trust and helps create constituencies for the data. However, rigidity can be deadly, especially in the face of administrative or other transcendent changes.

It is wise to align and calibrate population indicators and program performance measures with the initiatives and strategies of a new administration. Don't be afraid to try new measures, report formats, or continuous improvement approaches. Consider your report documents to be "living" documents.

Sometimes a change in "look and feel" is all a new administration needs to feel like they are putting their stamp on things. Don't get us wrong – we are not denigrating the improvement efforts of new administrations – but we are suggesting that in order to sustain the data-driven culture that has taken hold in an organization, a new administration needs to "see itself' in the data approaches and products. This can sometimes be accomplished without radical changes to those approaches or products.

Integrate New Approaches

Sometimes a new administration will come with new ideas and approaches, or entire measurement/continuous improvement frameworks that they want to implement in the organization. In an organization where a lot of progress has been made instilling a data-driven culture, it can be tempting to resist such changes. DON'T. Don't get so stuck in your current framework that you lose the potential value of new approaches. The trick is to, if necessary, adopt the new framework while maintaining the key elements of the prior approaches. There is no need to throw out prior good work. Most manifestations of performance and/or continuous improvement frameworks are in some ways hybrid approaches, borrowing from multiple conceptual frameworks and using multiple tools. This is okay. Be responsive to a new administration's favored approaches – usually there are some good elements you can incorporate. As the Vogons say in *The Hitchhiker's Guide to the Galaxy*, "resistance is useless."[9] Adapt, incorporate, hybridize, and sustain!

Notes

1 Friedman, Mark, *Trying Hard Is Not Good Enough*. Sante Fe, New Mexico: Trafford Press, 2006.
2 Hatry, Harry, *Performance Measurement: Getting Results*. Washington, DC: Urban Institute, 2006.

3 Tufte, Edward, *The Visual Display of Quantitative Information.* Cheshire, CT: Graphics Press, 1983.
4 Holzer, Marc and Ballard, Andrew (editors), *The Public Productivity and Performance Handbook,* 3rd Edition. London: Routledge, 2022.
5 See Friedman and Hatry.
6 McIntyre-Lahner, Anne. *Stop Spinning Your Wheels: Using Results-Based Accountability to Steer Your Agency to Success.* 4th Quadrant, 2016.
7 Schack, Ronald, *Confessions of a Data Scientist…or Warrior Priest: Lessons from 25 Years of Data Science, Performance Measurement, and Decision Support.* Morrisville: Lulu Press, 2019.
8 Cohen, March, and Olsen, 1972. The garbage can theory of organizational choice. *Administrative Science Quarterly,* Vol. 17, No. 1, pp. 1–25.
9 Adams, Douglas, *The Hitchhiker's Guide to the Galaxy.* New York: DelRay, 1979.

12

Data Fear and the Application of Evidence-Based and Promising Practices

We believe that evidence-based and promising practices are a very positive addition to our data analytic and accountability toolbox. In this section, we will discuss the benefits of evidence-based and promising practices and will also discuss some common problematic issues with using evidence-based and promising practices and how that can affect individuals and organizations dealing with data fear. "Evidence-based" is an important, and often misunderstood, term. Let's look at what makes something an evidence-based practice:

Evidence-based means that strong evidence exists to demonstrate a specific service or service delivery method. The evidence includes that the program or practice:

- Delivers the desired results for the population for whom it has been designed
- Has specific and well-defined components
- Can be replicated by staff teams other than the team that designed, or originally delivered, the service
- Has been evaluated using a scientifically designed process, that often includes a randomized control trial (RCT)

DOI: 10.4324/9781003496328-17

◆ Additionally, the process for becoming Evidence-based is a standardized one that is administered by a government agency or recognized practitioner organization so that an independent and unbiased process exists. In other words, to be truly considered evidence-based, an organization cannot just determine that its services are evidence-based because it gets good outcomes or because it has developed a program based on what it believes to be sound ideas. The service type itself must have been through the process discussed above.

Developing Data Practitioners

It is important to understand that a randomized control trial (RCT) means that some individuals will be randomly assigned into a group to receive the service being tested, and some will be randomly assigned to a group that does not receive the service. Oftentimes, those who don't get the service will be assigned to receive "treatment as usual" or the services that existed before the service being tested existed. Sometimes they won't get service. Also, be aware that an RCT is not something that is usually done every year… but routine measurement data, often supporting the same measures used in an RCT, can be collected and reported whenever such services are provided. Thus, once an RCT evaluation study is conducted, it can and should inform routine performance measurement efforts.

Another, similar term is "Promising Practice." A promising practice is a practice or service that

◆ Can reasonably be expected to deliver the desired results for the population for whom it has been designed
◆ Has specific and well-defined components
◆ Can be replicated by staff teams other than the team that designed or originally delivered the service

The difference between a promising practice and an evidence-based practice is that a promising practice has not been evaluated using a scientifically designed process. There can be plenty of reasons why programs/practices haven't been through the scientific testing process:

- There is an objection to going through the scientific process – especially an RCT – because that means that, by design, some people will not get the services believed to work the best
- The program is so small that there will not be enough evidence even after going through the process
- The program is new or just hasn't yet completed the process to become evidence-based

Benefits to Using Evidence-Based and Promising Practices

There are some important benefits to using evidence-based and promising practices. They include:

- Participants have a realistic opportunity to benefit from services that use an approach that has been proven to work instead of receiving services that are popular because they are willing to take all referrals– even if they are unqualified to serve them
- Investing in services that work or are likely to work is a good use of public or philanthropic dollars
- These programs offer a real opportunity for real system effectiveness by delivering good outcomes for clients
- Promising practices offer a new approach to service delivery, or a new supplement to service delivery, that some early evidence suggests can make a real difference in outcomes
- Some types of programs have lagging outcomes, and it can be difficult to collect and report data on such outcomes in a regular and timely way. Evidence-based practices, when implemented with fidelity, can allow for the use of intermediate outcome data as a proxy for more distal outcomes while data on more lagging measures are collected because there is evidence that application of such programs results in better outcomes.

Things to Be Aware of When Considering Evidence-Based and Promising Practices

There are also some realistic challenges and concerns about using evidence-based and promising practices. They include:

◆ The population on which an evidence-based service is established or tested may not be the same as the population being served in a particular program.[1] Many programs and practices are developed for, and tested on, middle-class white individuals or families; however, the individuals and families referred to the services may have racial and/or cultural backgrounds, and language barriers and related service needs, that are different than the population on which the service was tested. These differences bring into question whether the service is actually effective for the population receiving the service. This can also be true due to differences in the service environment or geography, or both; a particular approach may work in an urban setting but may be less effective in a rural setting, or some feature of the practice may be more effective in certain geographies than others due to geography-based differences (such as a different mix of industries).

◆ A true evidence-based practice has been through a rigorous external process before being determined to be evidence-based. Some practitioners call their services evidence-based based on the practitioner's belief that they have evidence that their program works; therefore, they call it evidence-based. Watch out for this kind of claim. The service in question may work well, but if it hasn't been through a process like the one described above, it cannot be considered evidence-based.

◆ Some practitioners compare their existing practices to actual evidence-based practices, determine that they are doing something similar, and identify their services as evidence-based. It is not accurate to relabel the existing practices as evidence-based. They must go through the evaluation and vetting by the appropriate authority to determine that the program is evidence-based.

◆ Some practitioners will combine elements from multiple evidence-based services or programs and put them together into a new service, and call the new service evidence-based. Although this is a tempting idea, combining parts of multiple evidence-based programs does not necessarily equal a new evidence-based program; the new combinations of elements need to be tested and vetted to ensure that they work as well in combination as they do in the original programs.

◆ It is also problematic when programs that have strong evidence of good outcomes (and may one day be certified as evidence-based) are defunded, or terminated based on a funder's desire to only fund evidence-based programs. If we only ever use and fund evidence-based programs, we will never develop new programs based on new thinking. It is important to test out programs that appear to work, and if they don't pass the evidence-based test, either modify and strengthen them and test them again, or replace them only after having developed good evidence that, in fact, they don't provide reliably consistent outcomes.

◆ Finally, it is possible to rely too much on a program's evidence-based label, even when your eyes and the data tell you the program is not delivering expected outcomes. Practitioners of evidence-based services are not all equally strong and don't always follow the service delivery model or deliver services to the population for whom the model was developed. It is important to continue to assess progress for yourself, and when a model doesn't work as designed, find out why. Question the practitioner, and maybe even the model developer. Refreshingly, many (although not all) developers of evidence-based and promising practices welcome discussions about the effectiveness and appropriateness of their model. They want to make sure services are being delivered correctly, and if they can learn something to strengthen their model, they will often embrace the challenge. In short, do not assume that just because a service carries the designation of evidence-based, it is automatically the correct and most effective service for you to utilize.

We have discussed both problematic issues with using evidence-based services and positive reasons for using them, and we truly believe that evidence-based and promising practices are a very positive addition to our toolbox. Our cautions can be divided into two main categories:

The first caution is making sure we use evidence-based services correctly– the right service for the right population;

The second caution is making sure that a service that is labeled as evidence-based is truly evidence-based and not a combination, or copycat, or untested service being touted as evidence-based.

If you understand what evidence-based and promising practices truly mean and are careful to follow the guidelines outlined above, you should find that you are able to use evidence-based and promising practices with strong success.

Data Fears Related to Evidence-Based Practices

We won't be able to measure whether we are doing the evidence-based practice correctly.

A: Evidence-based practices are designed and distributed with performance measures that are identified by the developer. Most of those measures are related to "fidelity to the model" or– whether you are implementing the program correctly. The focus on quality is a good thing in many ways; and it can also be somewhat frustrating for people who are equally interested in outcomes for their clients. The thinking behind the focus on model fidelity is that since the program has been scientifically shown to work when implemented correctly, the most important thing for program operators and funders to measure is whether the program was implemented with fidelity, because then they should achieve the outcomes identified by the model developers. We believe there are a lot of assumptions inherent in that kind of thinking, and that, in the same way that we discussed the importance of making sure we understand the source data when considering data visualizations (i.e., are the visualizations telling us what we think they are telling us), it is important to examine similar issues with evidence-based programs (i.e., is the program being delivered as planned and for the population it was planned for). This is where you can use your enlightened ignorance and your personal knowledge bank to continue asking questions and engage in the types of conversations we described above.

Take a minute to think about, and write down, some questions you would want to know about an evidence-based practice.

Here are some questions we think make sense to ask:

What is the program developer's target population for this service, and is our target population the same? (And are we actually serving our target population?)

If we are serving the intended population, are we implementing the program with fidelity?

If we are serving the right population, and implementing services with fidelity, are we seeing the outcomes we expect?

If yes to all of the above, then good! If the answer is "no" to one or more of those questions, start thinking about the additional information you need to know, and the kind of data you will want to look at to get a better understanding of how the program is faring.

We won't be able to quantitatively establish that the evidence-based practice is working for our target population.

A: This is an opportunity for you to put your enlightened ignorance and your personal knowledge bank to work, just like in the previous question. Going through the process we suggested in the last question should help you get to the evidence you are looking for.

It is important to note that it is possible you may find out the program is not working for your target population. That is just as important as finding out that it does work, because it empowers you to use your knowledge to either fix the program or change program models to one that actually works for your clients.

It is also important to note that it feels very scary to identify something that doesn't work. This is one of those times that you may want to confer with a trusted colleague who can help you feel confident in your analysis of the data, and in your conclusions. When you find that your conclusions are correct, remember that finding out that something is not working as planned is very important and can be very beneficial to your constituents and to your organization.

We won't be able to establish that our program, which has many elements in common with an established evidence-based practice, is similar enough to that practice to use the evidence-based practice as an argument for the continuation of our program.

A: You are correct– good catch on that one! As we wrote earlier in this section, you cannot claim your program is evidence-based because you believe it is similar enough to an established evidence-based program. You would need to go through the process of establishing it as evidence-based. That process differs slightly based on the type of programming and funding source for your program. There are multiple online resources you can access that describe evidence-based services and the related processes; they are generally organized by the type of service being provided (ex. behavioral health, juvenile justice, criminal justice, positive youth development).

However, if you have a strong program description, a clear target population, and good data that indicate your program is making a difference for the people you serve, you may be able to argue that your program is a promising practice. Depending on the factors we discussed earlier in this section, it may make sense for you to begin the process of becoming evidence-based. At a minimum, if you are concerned about ongoing funding for your program, the data that show your program works for your target population will make a strong argument to a funder.

Our program is not evidence-based, but we know it is achieving good outcomes. How do we hold our ground on our current approach in the face of pressure to adopt a popular evidence-based practice?

A. Use the data to show the program is achieving those good outcomes! As we wrote earlier, you don't have to get fancy to show how well your program is performing. A simple chart that shows basic program performance should suffice. We like to show measures that highlight the quantity of work being performed (ex., the number of clients you serve, the number of services you deliver), the quality of that work (ex., staff qualifications, cost of service, client satisfaction), and– most importantly– whether you are making a difference for your clients[2] (client outcomes).

As we described in our answer to the last question, if your program has a strong program description, a clear target population, and good data that indicate your program is making a difference for the people you serve, you may be able to argue that your program is a promising practice. It may also make sense for you to consider going through the process of becoming evidence-based. Either way, let the data help you hold your ground, and remember to contextualize your data with the story that goes along with it by explaining the positive and negative forces that impact your performance.

Notes

1 See Pawson, *Evidence-based Policy: A Realist Perspective*. London: SAGE, 2006.

2 Developed from Friedman, Mark, *Trying Hard Is Not Good Enough*. Santa Fe, New Mexico: FPSI, 2005, 2015.

13

Community Data Fear and Data Responsibility

Now, more than ever before, there is a clear recognition that accessing and using data gives the user power. Power to understand, power to persuade, and power to act. The approaches discussed above can place data power in the hands of individuals, more quickly and easily, than would have been thought possible only a few years ago. Placing that data power into the hands of individuals empowers them and can democratize the analysis and decision processes. As access to that power is created, it is critical that those accessing such power also understand the responsibilities that come with it.

We think it is important to emphasize the following elements of responsibility as access to data is provided:

Knowing your data: ensuring that you fully understand the data elements you are working with, including how data elements have changed over time.

Avoiding data selectivity: use all the data, not just the data that make your case.

Acknowledge differences in program types, sites, and the customer mix when making comparisons; sometimes comparisons are not appropriate at all.

DOI: 10.4324/9781003496328-18

Avoiding over-reliance on averages when data for sub-populations, sub-groups, or different sites may be very different.

Avoiding emphasizing momentary changes in trend data, when those changes can just be noise

Avoiding misleading data displays; including displays with truncated scales and displays that are intentionally obtuse.

Knowing the statistical methods you are using. Just because you can push on an icon and produce lots of output, doesn't mean you should if you can't interpret the output.

Validate results. Check your insights for consistency with prior findings; ask others to look at your logic and findings with a critical eye before "going live" with results.

Cite Sources. Honestly.

Adhere to privacy and confidentiality protections. Seriously.

14

Data Fear and DEIA (Diversity, Equity, Inclusion, and Accessibility)

On his first day in office, President Biden issued an executive order promoting diversity, equity, inclusion, and accessibility. The order defines each of the four terms as follows[1]:

♦ The term "diversity" means the practice of including the many communities, identities, races, ethnicities, backgrounds, abilities, cultures, and beliefs of the American people, including underserved communities.

♦ The term "equity" means the consistent and systematic fair, just, and impartial treatment of all individuals, including those who belong to underserved communities that have been denied such treatment.

♦ The term "inclusion" means the recognition, appreciation, and use of the talents and skills of employees of all backgrounds.

♦ The term "accessibility" means the design, construction, development, and maintenance of facilities, information and communication technology, programs, and services so that all people, including people with disabilities, can fully and independently use them. Accessibility includes

DOI: 10.4324/9781003496328-19

the provision of accommodations and modifications to ensure equal access to employment and participation in activities for people with disabilities, the reduction or elimination of physical and attitudinal barriers to equitable opportunities, a commitment to ensuring that people with disabilities can independently access every outward-facing and internal activity or electronic space, and the pursuit of best practices such as universal design.

There are many variations of these definitions. Randall Pinkett describes diversity as "the range of human differences," equity as "fairness and equality in outcomes" and inclusion as "involvement and empowerment."[2] He further suggests that progress in these areas results in belonging, or "feeling valued, heard, and accepted."[3]

In recent years, there has been increased public awareness and concern regarding the extent to which public programs foster and support the above principles. It doesn't take much imagination to envision the fear associated with actually determining the extent to which an organization and/or its programs are making progress in these areas. The fear might be related to doubting one's skill in calculating the measures correctly, or it might be related to how the data will be used once it is shared.

Some important, potentially fear-laden questions might immediately come to mind when considering measuring DEIA:

◆ How would we even measure whether this was happening or not?
◆ What if the data show that we are not achieving diversity, inclusion, equity, or accessibility? What do we do about that? Will revealing these things open ourselves up to lawsuits or other legal challenges?
◆ How could we expect to overcome systematic biases built into programs, organizations, and systems?

Efforts to measure and analyze DEIA must start with an acknowledgement that it is important and appropriate to devote resources to such efforts. That is where the fear comes in. Unlike other organizational measures that may be routinely reviewed, if these areas have not been measured, there is uncertainty about what such measures would show. We may even have a feeling that it may not be very positive, which can lead to avoidance– "Once we know about it, we have to do something about it...."

These questions also touch on foundational issues like systemic racism and implicit bias, which are very sensitive and are often politicized. This serves to exacerbate fear about "going down that road" to actually measure and start to systematically try to improve these conditions. Addressing such fear can start by learning how to talk about these issues in an open and transparent way, **acknowledging one's own potential for implicit bias**. We recommend obtaining some **formal training** designed to explore and understand such potential biases. At the organizational level, **executive-level sponsorship** of such efforts is critical...it is difficult to initiate such measurement efforts without it.

Like other measurement efforts we have described, once measurement of these areas is initiated, there has to be a **systematic process for reviewing the data** and developing strategies for improvement. It is important to go through an **adequate diagnostic process** when problems are identified and not leap to easy or common solutions. Strategies should be accompanied by an **appropriate theory of change** (how will actions related to this strategy contribute to improving this particular measure). Given that these areas may not have been fully considered by the organization previously, this is also an area where **best practice research** and **technical assistance** are appropriate. Setting targets for improvement can be helpful; actually stating a goal, that is communicated program or organization-wide, that we want to improve particular DEIA measures by x percent by x time, helps communicate the importance of improving these measures to staff and clients alike.

Measuring DEIA

Measuring **diversity** seems like a straightforward thing:

1. Define your universe (an organization, program, system, or community)

2. Identify the types of groups/categories you want to measure (gender, race, ethnicity, age, sexual orientation, disability status, veteran status...there may be others as well)
3. Adopt (or create) a specific operational definition for diversity
4. Determine the degree of representation of those groups in the defined universe (usually expressed as a percentage)
5. Compare that degree of representation with some desired state, and calculate the difference
6. Once a baseline is established, periodically re-measure to determine progress.

The devil, of course, is in the details...how the universe is defined, what groups are chosen and how they are defined, how the degree of representation is calculated, whether and how it is disaggregated, and what and how the desired state is defined. An organization, collaborative, or community conducting such comparative analyses has to work through these issues, which could become quite contentious. Of course, many of us fear conflict, so even embarking on a discussion like this might instill fear in those attempting to begin such an analysis.

Measuring **equity,** too, seems like a relatively straight-forward endeavor:

1. Determine what activity, service, or outcome you are investigating from an equity perspective, and identify how you count or measure the activity, service, or outcome of interest
2. Identify the types of groups/categories you want to measure (gender, race, ethnicity, age, sexual orientation, disability status, veteran status...there may be others as well)
3. Adopt (or create) a specific operational definition for equity
4. Disaggregate the measure of the activity, service, or outcome by the different groups of interest, and

5. Compare the outcomes for those groups with those not in those groups. This can be a comparison of the percentage of the target groups achieving outcomes with the percentage of other individuals achieving outcomes. Likelihood ratios are also sometimes used, showing the likelihood that a member of a particular target group will achieve (or not achieve) an outcome, compared with the likelihood that other individuals will achieve that outcome
6. Once a baseline is established, periodically re-measure to determine progress

Again, what is easy becomes hard. What activities, services, or outcomes are the most important ones to measure? What groups are chosen, and how are they defined? Are the data elements that allow for appropriate disaggregation even available? If differences are found, how do we know whether the differences are practically significant?

Inclusion may be the hardest to measure, in that we tend to lack systematically collected data on inclusion (involvement and empowerment) in most organizations. However, the steps are straight-forward:

1. Adopt (or create) a definition for inclusion, and define the ways in which inclusion (that is, group members feeling like they are involved and empowered) is demonstrated in an organization, program, or system
2. Measures of involvement in particular processes or decisions can be used here. One way to do that is to ask group members to report the degree to which they are involved or empowered on those dimensions (often using a survey tool)
3. Analyze differences in average responses for those of different groups
4. Barriers or challenges to increased empowerment or involvement on different dimensions may be asked about in the same survey instrument
5. Once a baseline is established, periodically re-measure to determine progress

Again, the difficulty here is that not all organizations regularly collect this information. Sufficient organizational attention and resources need to be allocated in order to initiate such data collection efforts, including the development of valid survey instruments, administering the surveys, analyzing the data, reviewing the data, and coming up with strategies to foster and improve inclusion.

Accessibility is another category where data are usually not systematically collected. There are also specific legal provisions, such as the Americans with Disabilities Act (ADA), that stipulate the kinds of access and accommodations that should serve as the baseline for accessibility improvement efforts. As such, the measurement steps include:

1. Identify the specific dimensions of accessibility that are critical to measure (ADA and related provisions within specific program legislation (e.g., the Workforce Investment and Opportunity Act). Checklists of important provisions can be readily obtained
2. Develop a method for determining whether and to what extent the organization is complying with these provisions (often, an audit approach is used–this can be a self-assessment, a peer review, or a formal monitoring approach from a funder)
3. Develop appropriate measures to show progress. For example, the number and percent of provisions that are not in compliance, in partial compliance, or in full compliance
4. Ask clients the extent to which they feel they are being adequately accommodated and supported, and how those accommodations can be improved
5. Once a baseline is established, periodically re-measure to determine progress

Using the above approach can serve to mitigate some of the fear associated with measuring DEIA. Being transparent with such data is also important. It shows the organization is serious about addressing these concerns and is taking steps to improve.

However, this can lead to fears related to use…fear that the data will be used against the organization, or that the data will be misinterpreted. Always reporting such data with a "story behind the baseline" is critical; it allows the organization to provide their own interpretation of what the current state is and to simultaneously show that steps are being taken to address the problem and mitigate these risks, helping to ameliorate those fears.

Notes

1 https://www.whitehouse.gov/briefing-room/presidential-actions/2021/06/25/executive-order-on-diversity-equity-inclusion-and-accessibility-in-the-federal-workforce/
2 Pinkett, Randall, *Data Driven DEI*. Hoboken, NJ: Wiley, 2023.
3 Pinkett, ibid.

15

The Promise and Perils of the Use of Artificial Intelligence in Data Analysis and Reporting

We hear about the promise of artificial intelligence (AI) on a daily basis. AI can assist with data analysis and reporting in many different ways, but it may also trigger fear of the unknown and fear of loss of control, and both individuals and organizations may experience "crossover" fears (the intersection of fears related to capacity and fears related to use of data) when considering the use of AI.

AI can assist with data analysis and reporting in multiple ways. Analysts can use AI to automate the process of data cleaning, dealing with problems like missing values, outliers, and helping to standardize data formats. Data from multiple sources can also be integrated using AI tools - bringing multiple data sets together to create a more comprehensive picture of what is being analyzed.

Pattern recognition is a particular strength of AI. AI models can also help with pattern recognition…processing vast amounts of data to detect patterns, relationships between variables, and detecting potentially significant anomalies in data sets.

Analysts can also benefit from the use of AI-driven tools to produce better data summaries and visualizations of complex

DOI: 10.4324/9781003496328-20

data sets. These tools can also be helpful in creating regular, automated reports – creating tables, charts, and even basic narrative explanations. These tools can also be made interactive, allowing for the automatic grouping or disaggregation of data… other foundations of data analysis. These approaches can often reduce errors in reporting as well as ease the reporting burden, thereby allowing us humans to focus on what the data mean and better inform decision-making.

AI can help data analysts identify the correct methods for a particular analysis and provide actual code that can be implemented to conduct the analysis. For example, Ron was recently trying to determine how to implement a fixed effects regression model, but needed some clarity about what variables should be "fixed." He described what he wanted to do in an AI tool, and the tool provided him with the insight he needed, and the code he needed to use in order to correctly implement the analysis.

Of course, AI has become well known for producing pre-dictive models, forecasts, and time series analysis that can make data-driven predictions based on historical data. These models, if developed using good data, can be of great use to organizations trying to forecast future trends or determine the potential via-bility of proposed solutions.

Qualitative data analysis can also be supported by AI tools: using natural language processing, AI tools can look at open-ended text, summarize it, or categorize it, and even con-duct "sentiment analysis" to identify the preferences or opinions of respondents. This can be very useful to analysts who have to cull through large amounts of qualitative information and make sense of it.

Generative AI can also help with identifying different dimensions or domains of research, generate qualitative inter-view or survey questions, or even serve as a sort of meta-analytic aggregator of data findings for use in benchmarking or identifi-cation of promising or best practices.

As with many cases of data fear, there are some legitimate concerns or risks that may need to be mitigated. One pervasive fear is that you cannot see into the "black" box of AI algorithms. Even if you can actually review the code and the inputs into the models, they can be challenging to understand. This lack of transparency can instill uncertainty and doubt related to the use of AI in decision-making.

A related fear relates to the possibility that AI algorithms may inherit biases present in the data used to "train" the AI model. These biases may be subtle and hard to detect but can influence the output of the AI models and may have real-world consequences.

Like a lot of technological applications, there can be serious privacy concerns. AI algorithms can and do analyze large datasets, which may contain sensitive information about individuals. Unauthorized access or misuse of this data can lead to privacy violations and breaches. Similarly, like most technological systems, AI systems can be vulnerable to attacks, including adversarial attacks where malicious actors manipulate data to mislead AI system results. These can be very difficult to detect.

Probably the largest concern with an AI data analysis application is data quality...garbage in, garbage out applies. If AI models are applied to data that are not of good quality, the output of these models can be suspect.

Another concern with the application of AI to data analysis is that it becomes a solution in search of a problem. Not every analysis warrants the application of a "heavy-duty" AI application. Sometimes, a simple table or chart, developed in a basic spreadsheet application like Microsoft Excel or Google Sheets, can give an organization what it needs, without getting bogged down with identifying the correct AI tool, or investing time or resources in setting up an automated AI process, for something that could be done in a straightforward, non-AI way. Also, sometimes it is easier to gain buy-in for an analysis if it is done in a way that can be readily explained in a transparent, easy-to-understand way. As mentioned earlier, many AI applications are less than transparent...and therefore may generate a degree of skepticism and mistrust. Like many other aspects of public administration, the correct solution is one that is sustainable, and also appropriately scaled to the task at hand. Analytic approaches should be calibrated to the nature and importance of the analysis.

Beyond the above concerns, over reliance on AI can serve to reduce other non-AI analytic capacity in an organization. This can create problems when an organization needs to conduct analysis without using an AI tool. As AI approaches become more prevalent, organizations of course will want to develop the capacity to use those approaches and hire people who know how to implement them. However, it will be critical for organizations to retain those who can conduct analyses without being "tethered" to AI tools (or any specific tool, for that matter), to ensure the organization continues to be flexible, adaptive, and can pivot when necessary.

Before Implementing AI in an Organization

When considering the use of an AI tool, some of the questions an organization should ask include:

Do we really need to use AI? Is the task something that really doesn't warrant an AI "intervention?"

Do we understand what logic the AI tool is using? Can we explain it in everyday language?

Do we know what data the AI tool was trained on? Are there any biases in those data that we should be aware of?

How will we ensure that the AI tool does not violate any confidentiality or privacy concerns?

How will the output of the tool be reviewed and validated?

When using generative AI, how can we ensure that it hasn't missed or omitted important considerations?

How are we going to utilize the output of the AI tool? Will the output be integrated with other data and information to provide context (and perhaps balance) to the AI output?

Answering these questions will go a long way in developing a "risk mitigation" strategy for the application of AI tools for data analysis and reporting. This can serve to ameliorate data fear related to AI associated with how AI output might be used or the risks associated with it. As we mentioned at the beginning of this chapter, there may also be fear of AI associated with capacity. The foundations of AI are technical, and one can easily be lost in jargon, buzzwords, and the strangeness of working with something that seems so different and complex. Fear associated with not really understanding what the tool is doing, and awe that it is doing it – "I can't believe the AI tool generated such an elaborate response so well...and so fast!" –may make individuals and organizations shy away from AI, or be critical of its use when such criticism may not be warranted.

AI is definitely here for good...and like data more generally, organizations cannot afford to ignore the promise of AI. As you embark on your AI journey, do so with open eyes. Remember, AI was created by humans, imperfect creatures that we are, and nothing created by humans is infallible or bullet-proof.

If you are experiencing fear reactions at the thought of implementing AI in your organization, we suggest taking the following steps

1. start with the anxiety-busting tools we have discussed in this book.
2. Once individuals can move toward the fear of AI, the next step is learning; get some good sources on how AI works...how models are developed, how they are trained, and the different kinds of applications available.
3. Take baby steps. Get one of the basic AI tools and start to work with it.
   a) See for yourself how an AI tool can create a chart, or generate a narrative
   b) Think about how you might use it in your organization.
   c) Talk to other organizations that use AI – ask them what their experience has been
   d) Get some technical assistance from peers and/or other experts

Q and A Conversation:

Q: If artificial intelligence can perform all these functions, is it really necessary for my colleagues and me to learn how to use data ourselves? Can't we just delegate it to an AI program?

A: These systems need to be established in any organization before they can be used, and they need to be "connected" to the relevant data. That might occur over time, but even after AI is used for some data in an organization, it might not be easily connected to the data that a particular unit or staff person needs to analyze. So, it is important to retain data analytic skills within the organization, even after such systems start to be used.

Q: I have read some articles in the news about how AI makes mistakes, or just makes up facts. How do I know when it is working right, and when it is making mistakes?

A: If you are connecting AI tools to organizational data, you can also do an independent analysis of the same data to determine how consistent the AI tool output is with the "non-AI" analysis. Some things to check for, include making sure it is not biased, and is not missing important analytic elements. If you find the output of a tool is generating biased, inaccurate, or incomplete answers, don't use that tool!

Q: Since it seems like AI knows more about data than my colleagues and I, how do we know how to ask it questions, give it tasks, and monitor what it is doing?

A: You need to identify what you want to know, and ask AI the right questions. Learning to ask the right questions of data is part of the data comfort/data literacy journey. You need to have the answers checked by people doing the actual work… and check to see whether the "AI answers" pass the "sniff test." This should be done regularly. AI tools are great…but not infallible, and routinely monitoring and validating the output of AI is a critical task. You don't need to understand the technical details of how AI arrives at its answers, but you do need to consistently evaluate its output. This may be a good place to reach out to your data mentor for some additional assistance.

New Data Practitioners

As we have written before, change comes in baby steps. As you begin to develop an awareness of AI tools and begin to make forays into their use, consider working with your data mentor(s) for direction, guidance, and risk management. Don't expect that you will become an expert at all facets of working with data overnight. Learning and experimenting are good – don't jeopardize your newfound confidence by taking on too much, too soon.

16

An Interview with the Authors

We sat down together to talk about why we wrote this book, some of our experiences with data and how we both have evolved on our data journeys.

ANNE: Ron, in your book, *Confessions of a Data Scientist...or Warrior Priest?* you describe yourself as a data scientist. When did you start identifying yourself as a data scientist? What prompted you to describe yourself that way?

RON: Great question. Not easy to answer. I first heard the term data scientist maybe 8 or 9 years ago. It may have been used before then, but that was the first time I heard it. I immediately liked it, because it captures what I do: use data to better understand the world. Now I know that sometimes the term data scientist is more narrowly construed, to mean someone who is using machine learning or artificial intelligence approaches in order to develop information for action, but I disagree with this, because it seems like the purveyors of a few particular methods have inappropriately appropriated a term that can apply to lots of different methods and approaches. The reason I like the term data scientist is that it could be used more generally....and it describes what I do better than a lot of other things that people, including myself, have called me over the years, like data analyst, program evaluator, or performance measurement consultant.

ANNE: I've heard you called a lot of things over the years...

DOI: 10.4324/9781003496328-21

RON: Yes, that is true (smiles).

RON: So that's why I used it. I used it as a book title because I wanted the book to sound current, but also because it truly captures what I do, which is to use data to understand the world.

What about you? Do you consider yourself a data scientist?

ANNE: I don't. I don't at all. And honestly, it wasn't until a few years ago when I got into the RBA work and started working with you and a couple of our colleagues, that I would even consider myself a data person. In fact, we would be in meetings together and I'd say, "I'm not a data person," and you guys would tell me to "stop saying that, because you sound disingenuous – you use data a lot." I had to sit back and realize, wow – I've gone from someone who shied away from data and just wanted to do those touchy groovy helpy things...to realizing that in order to make a difference doing those touchy groovy helpy things, I really needed to understand what worked and what didn't work, who I was really working with, and who benefited from things and who didn't benefit from things. So I am now at a point where I consider myself a data person. I think I fall into the continuum of more among...I represent all those people who do not yet feel empowered as a data person, because that is where I came from. I feel like my role in the data world, or the data person world is to open up the doors...and say, "you don't need to be a data scientist...we like our data scientist friends, but to be a good data person you don't have to be a data scientist, so come on in....you need to be a data person."

RON: That's really cool. And I guess even though I use this general definition of "using data to understand the world," if you were to compare that with a more general term like "data person" or "person who regularly uses data," I guess I would have to modify [my definition] to say "person who uses scientific methods with data to understand the world."

Those would include some of the more technical aspects of applying the scientific method – the statistical approaches involved and the different predictive methods you might use – which include things like machine learning....

ANNE: But is not limited to that...

RON: Right. It's not limited to that. It encompasses a lot of different things like basic data visualization, statistical tests, regression analysis, stuff like that...but also things like geographic information analysis – placed based analysis – all of those tools come into play in trying to understand the world – and I guess the data scientist part of me is the part who uses those technical tools to understand the world.

ANNE: That's cool. That leads me to another question. When we were working on this book, probably a few months ago at this point, you told me you were not always a data person. And that really surprised me...because when I talk about you to other colleagues that I am going to introduce you to, I say, "he's like my favorite data nerd," and "he's great at all that technical stuff," so when you ever told me that you weren't always a data person, I was really surprised. Could you remind me what the story was – why weren't you always a data person? And what changed? When did you become one?

RON: I'll try to do this without going on forever. In junior high and high school, I actually struggled with math. Part of that was it really didn't ring any bells for me...it wasn't very interesting. it just seemed like manipulating numbers in a way that didn't interest me very much. Because it didn't interest me, I didn't work very hard at it...so I didn't do very well. And, of course, that feeds on itself...if you don't do well in algebra, you won't do well in trig, and if you don't do well in trig, you won't do well in calculus...and on and on. By the time I got to college, I had a mindset of avoiding math courses when I could. If I didn't have to take any more math courses, I didn't.

It was a strange inconsistency because I always loved science. When I was a little kid my friend and I created a little pretend laboratory called CAT Labs (chemistry, astronomy, and technology), and throughout junior high and high school I liked science, but I was limited because of my math performance. But I still always liked science...but I avoided most science classes as an undergraduate too...because of my math issues. Except, I majored in philosophy in college, and I took this really cool course in symbolic logic...which was really a math course in sheep's clothing. And I did really well in that… and I think that was the start of saying, I can do this stuff…and if it interests me I kind of get better at it.

By the time I got to grad school, I had a real purpose for the math I was trying to do. And that purpose was to understand the world….I made the connection in my head about doing math so that I could solve problems that mattered to me and that mattered to the world. A lot of that had to do with doing policy analysis, making programs more effective, and creating better policies. I ended up taking a lot of math in grad school, playing catch up a little bit…but I realized that I didn't have a faulty math gene. So, I ended up taking a lot of math and other data-related courses. So that's how I changed. That interest in improving government programs and performance measurement was because I had a parallel thing going with what I was doing in school and what I was doing for work at the labor department, where there had been a big reorganization and there was a big emphasis on total quality management and on performance measurement. When those things converged it changed my whole outlook and world view on that stuff.

ANNE: Pretty neat…It became important, so you decided you had to do it. And you discovered you really could do it.

RON: There wasn't one moment where I decided I could do math now. It just kind of snuck up on me. Once I knew that I had some facility with math, all the latent scientific inclination that I had came back out. So that is my story and I'm sticking to it.

So…What about you? You said that you didn't think you were a data person or weren't a data person at first. So how did you look at math and data in your early career and even prior to that?

ANNE: I don't remember much about math before high school. I did pretty well…I remember having some hiccups with long division but got over that. I got into high school, and I started to have challenges with equations and algebra, and I didn't have the opportunity to ask questions and get help…things were not making sense to me. Like you said earlier, these things build on themselves…for me, I didn't really get algebra so I didn't get geometry which came next. And my family moved a lot due to career changes, so I moved from being right there, right in the math struggle, to moving; and the curriculum didn't line up from one school to another, and so I could sit at the sidelines...and then with the next move, I got into a "math for dummies" class. I exceled and was at the top of the class... but that didn't matter... I had tagged myself as a dummy as far as math went. I managed to mostly avoid most math in college. Even though one of my majors was experimental psychology, I didn't have to do a whole bunch of math. Then I went into the touchy groovy helpy work. I did have a summer job as a cost accounting clerk. I remember interviewing for the job and the guy asked, well...can you add? Can you subtract? Then you will be better than the last three people who had this job. Spending a summer doing math all summer long...it was pretty routine, and I was really good at it. That gave me some confidence. But I also knew I still was not a math person.

I was able to parley those really basic skills. In the mid-90s we started doing reports on kids in the juvenile justice system and how they were faring, and who were the kids in the juvenile justice system. I will never forget standing in my office, and numbers started to jump off the page at me. I remember having these great epiphanies about those data... it was like these weren't numbers, they were important information about how the system is working or not; working who gets put into this system and what happens to them, and who gets referred to the system. It was like a switch went on, and it has been on ever since.

RON: That's awesome!

At the Labor Department, I was hired as a hearing officer to decide whether people were eligible for unemployment or not. That really wasn't for me, and I transferred to the central office. I heard about this new unit they were creating called the performance measurement unit. In my graduate work, I had done a few stat courses and a computer applications course, so I knew about Lotus and Excel. I managed to get into that unit, but there was still a whole lot of stuff I didn't know. I knew a little bit about performance measurement, but I hadn't done too much real data analysis at that point. Over the next few years, I started to pick up multiple skills. I started to use Excel more and more and learned the power of spreadsheets... there's a lot you can do with spreadsheets. And, because we were doing customer satisfaction surveys at the department I started to use SPSS. This was the first time, other than a few class assignments, that I used a real stat software package to do frequency distributions and statistical tests and look at correlations in a real-world setting. In some ways there was an aspect of "diving in and doing it," ...I don't know if it was my relative youth at the time, or what, but I had very little reluctance to just try stuff. I think I still have some of that...I will try things out, and learn by doing.

ANNE: Do you ever experience data fear, anymore?

RON: Oh yeah. When I am interacting with people who might have a REALLY heavy quantitative background I can doubt my abilities. These people think in math terms...it's like the difference between someone who speaks a foreign language fluently and someone who understands but has to translate back and forth to English in their heads. I'm still that kind of a math guy...as opposed to someone who has equations running around in her head.

ANNE: I used to describe myself, and compare myself to other people as someone who "thinks in Word" as opposed to someone who "thinks in Excel." In terms of how you organize things, and "big ideas" and being able to organize and categorize ideas...Now, all of a sudden, I am bi-lingual...I think in Word and Excel. I realize I'm talking about Excel here, and not SPSS or R, but there is still a change. To a certain extent the more you use it, the more it makes sense and the more you can use it.

RON: One of the things that has made me successful over the years with this work is that I do tend to act as a translator, or a bridge between the really heavy quant guys...[this is all on a continuum of course, some people would look at me and say I'm a heavy quant guy, but there are some people I know that are in another universe as far as that goes]...not only the heavy quant guys but the really technical guys...the guys that write code all day...I've had many projects over the years where I am the one who takes the customer need and defines it in a technical enough way that the code guys can use that to develop their specifications.

How about you, do you experience data fear?

ANNE: Does the sun come up every morning? In our book, we talk about two kinds of data fear. One is fear about your own abilities and the other is fear about how data will be used. I guess I don't fear it so much anymore. It is that I doubt and question my abilities. When we do that imposter syndrome scale I'm like off the charts. You and I did a presentation a couple of years ago at the National Public Performance Conference in Boston. And I had some fun with it because one of the lines I got to use was pointing at the audience and saying, "you are a really scary group of people." I did that by talking about how non-data people perceive a group of public performance managers. It was empowering for me to point to them and say, "you are scary people"… because they scare me too…because of that whole imposter syndrome. I'm almost waiting for people to ask a question that I can't answer, or that I didn't have the foresight to think about, or that's going to show that I'm really not a data person and that I should go back to the touchy-feely groovy stuff. It happens less and less the more I am willing to put myself out there and the more I also realize that I know what I know, and there is a lot that I don't know. However, having said that, the stuff that I do know… I know pretty well. It's not that I want to "stay in my lane" and not branch out, but there are some things that I know in a data-related, or data and experience-related way that is as valid as anyone doing code or other technical stuff that I don't know that I could do. That's okay because I can appreciate that someone else can do that and that I can either understand it or go to my friend Ron who does that translation service, and I can get to a point where I understand it.

That is a long-winded way of saying I do experience data fear, and I also think that using data is so important that it's not a luxury I can afford anymore. I need to put that fear behind me and keep on moving forward realizing I know what I know, and that I am going to use that and put my fear behind me.

RON: I think that is really important and valuable to keep in mind. In addition to that, I think you would agree that we didn't write this book to try to convert the masses into little data scientists, or little "technical data wizzes." What we are trying to convey is that there is a world of data out there that can be really valuable to many people in their work, and if they just got over their basic hesitation about using and working with data they could really expand their skill set and their value to their organization and feel empowered about using data. I think there is nothing wrong with wanting to become a technical data wizard, and I would encourage anyone who is interested to pursue it...but that is not really what we are trying to do here. What we are trying to do is get people to find a way to be more comfortable with data so that they can use it to add value.

ANNE: Yes. All those people that like the "touchy groovy feely helpy" stuff...if you really want to do that or really want to help your population of focus or your clients or whoever it is you are trying to work with, help, empower, change...you need to be able to work with data enough that you can use it to empower them...you will not only become more valuable to yourself and your agency, you'll do a better job for the people you are trying to help.

RON: Right. As we talk about in the book, there are plenty of technical data people, or even people who might not really be all that technical but that use a lot of data buzz words, who – whether intentionally or not – make it harder for the "everyday Data Joe." There is a certain sense of power that people have when they use exclusive terms – buzz wordy terms that are hard to understand. Or use methods or applications...even if the methods aren't that sophisticated...if they are ones that take a little bit of knowledge--that other people don't have-- to use. I'll give an example – Using Tableau. Tableau is not all that technical to use, but if you haven't used it before – someone who uses Tableau says hey look at this... I can do this... – and you're going...well...I don't know...looks pretty cool...I don't know if I could do that...while not always intentional, sometimes that kind of use of a little bit of more knowledge than other people creates a power disparity. [intentional or not]... is something that we talk about and suggest using caution in those situations.

ANNE: I'll even take it a step further and say I firmly believe that there are people who use that little bit of extra data knowledge or data skill to [and I'm going to identify with the non-data masses] "put us back in our place" or "back in our lane." You leave that technical stuff to us...you keep on with that touchy groovy feely stuff...and we will tell you where you should be heading, we will tell you what the data mean. We have talked about this...this may be because those people have their own lack of confidence around whether or not they matter. Data people matter A LOT. A lot of people who are really good at data have a lot of other skills...they don't always have the skills to work with clients [some do], and it can be their way to emphasize their voice matters, or their contribution matters, just as much as you people working with the clients. What happens is it is really used to elevate themselves and put other people down. And if you are not confident in your data skills, it is easy to be pushed down.

RON: I think it gets worse. Sometimes there is almost a *veneration* of the technical stuff that is produced. That creates a positive feedback loop with the technical people. They get elevated because of the technical stuff they have produced. The non-data people are like "wow this is really good stuff," I could never do that... and it feeds into that whole pathology. Now, they deserve credit for what they do-don't get me wrong – but sometimes the praise combined with the exclusivity of their technical knowledge can go to their heads. I think that I have fallen into that trap over the years. Hearing how *good I am* at this performance stuff or this data stuff, I have to remind myself that "all glory is fleeting." [Laughs].

ANNE: You might feel that internally, but let me tell you, one of the things that has caused me to be able to identify as a data person is the fact that you have always been very open, and when I don't understand something you are able to explain it in common sense terms, using plain language that doesn't put me down, doesn't make me feel stupid and that empowers me.

You might be feeling "big" inside your head but on the outside, you are empowering people like me to be good data people.

RON: I guess that is what I mean by reminding myself about it… That's maybe why it doesn't come out that way to others. I am thinking, be careful about how you are representing yourself and how you say things…it matters.

ANNE: What is the most powerful use of data that you have been a part of?

RON: There are a lot of various data analyses that have pointed to real performance problems that have then been solved over the years…there is a lot of that. Recently I worked with my daughter on a social network analysis for the Hartford Police Department. We looked at how people who are arrested are associated with one another. They could be associated with one another because they were arrested together, or because they were arrested with someone who was arrested with another person so all three people over two different arrests were related. They could also be associated because they lived close together, or because the same two people knew a witness to a third crime. All these relationships were mapped out in what we call a social network analysis. We identified 7 people out of over 2,000 arrested for drug crimes, that had many, many more connections than the others that were arrested. So the Hartford Police were able to try to intervene with those people. They wouldn't have known to do that if we hadn't done this analysis. They would have had to sift through thousands of records manually, which wouldn't have happened.

ANNE: But you were able to use data reports?

RON: We used an arrest database, R, and a mapping software called Polinode. It was fun because I worked with my daughter, but also because the police were so appreciative…they found the analysis of such value that it had to warm the cockles of our hearts ☺

ANNE: I hope you are going to write that up!

RON: We are…I think Carolann and I are going to write this up. Particularly because we used a variable – that geographic proximity variable – that isn't usually used in social network analysis. So we are probably going to write that up.

How about you?

ANNE: There are two that really stand out to me. One I alluded to earlier, when I talked about all of a sudden really understanding the juvenile justice system. The other that ties for that is the work that I did at the CT Department of Children and Families-- which is actually how you and I met. We had a new commissioner who had committed to moving the agency into a data-informed and outcome-focused agency. She decided to use Results-Based Accountability. Because I was one of a few people in the agency who understood what RBA even meant, she tasked me with bringing our agency online being a RBA agency, which meant that we would switch our internal management practices and strategies, but also our contracted services (over 200 million dollars statewide) into measuring those services and whether or not they worked using this results-based approach – which is not very difficult and heavily reliant on data. It was teaching those touchy groovy feely helpy people and people who have been in a bureaucracy for many, many, years, that (1) they could do the data, and (2) they needed to use the data if they wanted to make the differences they were trying to make for the people they were serving. And I learned a tremendous amount, but I think I was able to contribute a fair bit with the process of getting a "social work-y" agency that used to measure performance with anecdotes, to begin to use data and use performance data to understand things a little bit differently and to start asking different questions designed to get honest answers…not necessarily flashy answers and not to make us look good…but to understand where the pain points were… to understand where we weren't doing so hot, and what was going on about that so that instead of telling this great story and these great anecdotes we could start to struggle with here's where we need to do better and to understand why, and what are the things we needed to do in order to do a better job. So that was important for my professional and personal growth, but also really important for the growth of a large agency and the thousands of families that they serve on a daily basis.

RON: This brings up something that is really important to remember when you talk about working with data. That is you don't work with data using these methods and approaches in a vacuum, you bring your whole package of reality and experiences into the application of those methods and approaches. So when you did that work, you weren't just applying RBA principles, you were doing project management, facilitation, and planning...bringing all those skills together with the data stuff you were applying. People have to remember that working with data leverages the other skills they have and brings them to a different level.

ANNE: The other piece of that is for all those people who work with clients or work with programs...that is really important too... when we talk about contextualizing data, and understanding the story about the data, and "why you got what you got" and what was going on...all that knowledge that people have about how people react to certain things...that doesn't get thrown out...we don't throw the baby out with the bathwater...we understand and value and utilize those important skills about our client population and services and how things work...we look at that with a data lens, and we look at the data with a program lens. So they are both super important.

RON: You can't do a performance diagnosis without context. You can't do a performance diagnosis without knowing how the service is being delivered, who the service is being delivered to, and what the services are. That is what the people doing the work can bring to the table.

ANNE: What kind of support do you have for your data work and what kinds of support do you think others need?

RON: At this point in my data journey, I still do a lot of stuff myself... including data entry. But there are times on big projects when I hire minions to do some of that work, that kind of basic data preparation work. So that's one kind of support. Sometimes, some data projects are pretty big and multi-dimensional and have a lot of different parts going on. I tend to enjoy quantitative data analytic work a lot. I like qualitative work too...but these days I let someone else do the qualitative analysis and then we bring it together. On the other end of the continuum,

I may farm out some of the really technical coding in things like R or Python, because I don't work with them enough in certain advanced ways to do it myself, nor do I have the time. But I am still in the center of all of it, bringing it together and using the elements to create a final report or product.

So, you have moved from your work in a state agency to being a consultant. How do you do that? How does work come to you...and what is your approach to the data world these days?

ANNE: Work comes to me in a couple of ways. One is putting myself out there...participating in meetings and workgroups and things that are important to me.....doing presentations. You put in plenty of time that you don't get paid for...but it's all part of kind of investing in that bigger picture...empowering other people. Sometimes that comes back to you and sometimes you have to feel good knowing that you got some good, important information out there in the bigger world. Work has come to me through participating in large projects. Work has come to me from other consultants who understand I have a certain type of expertise and a certain type of experience. I have worked for the non-profits and the state government. As far as program services go I have been on both sides of that equation...the performer and the performance analyzer. I have also done a good bit of teaching, which helps you think in a different way and approach the work in a different way. So a number of consultants have come to me and said look, we'd like your experience and expertise on this project. That's pretty neat, because then you are working with someone you know and they understand your strengths and you understand theirs, and you can find ways to complement each other strengths. You and I do that a lot and it's great fun and it's also really meaningful. I like being part of teams where we all complement each other. But then you also have to go out as an independent consultant and do extra work and respond to proposals and call people that you might not otherwise call and put yourself out there. That doesn't sound like the data part of the work, but I have come to realize that you have to have the data comfort that comes along with having at least

some of the data skills, to be able to say, yeah I can do that...
yes...you oughta fund me and here's why.

ANNE: How about you?

RON: I think you captured it...it's all of that stuff. At this point,
I've been a data consultant for 20 years. Over time ....of
course, once you work with a couple of agencies and different
organizations...you make connections that keep coming back
to you or refer you to other people. My company, the Charter
Oak Group, was lucky enough to work with the Connecticut
legislature for a ten-year period doing RBA. Through that process, we ended up connecting with 44 state agencies over the
course of that work...which of course was very beneficial to
us. There are also a lot of clients that you have for a long time...
there is the continued care and feeding of those clients...you
have to stay relevant for them, and show them new ways you
can add value for them...that social network analysis, for
example, or geographic information systems analysis...even
if it is doing a basic performance diagnosis in an area where
they hadn't applied it before...this helps you to stay relevant
with your current clients. When I wrote my book...I really
wrote that book for me...but I also thought it might help with
business development...I'm not sure it has...but that's ok too
[laughs]. On the other hand, being an author of a somewhat
technical book on data can't hurt. And like you, I have done
some teaching over the years. That to me helps establish some
credibility...but also, as you said, it is a different lens to look
at stuff through...it keeps you fresh when you have to look
at things differently and explain things differently to people.
All that stuff is cool.

RON: You made a name for yourself with Results Based
Accountability. Do you still feel connected with RBA? What
do you think about it now?

ANNE: I feel very connected to RBA. I remember when I first
learned about it and really started understanding it. At
that point I had been in non-profit and government jobs for
20 years. I remember learning about RBA and the focus on
outcomes, and the focus on using some pretty simple and
pretty straightforward data-oriented questions to figure out if

we were making a difference...it was like "wow I could have had a V8!" moment...it was, in a lot of ways, life-changing. A different way to look at the work. In that way, I feel extraordinarily connected and extraordinarily grateful for having been introduced to RBA, trained in RBA [including by the Charter Oak Group], and getting to do the RBA work in the time and place I was able to start doing that...because I continue doing the work.

What I have learned is that nothing is perfect...and there is no such thing as a panacea. RBA is my go-to framework for viewing the work and in many ways for viewing the whole human services world. I have been able to bring in some frameworks that I learned many years ago that still have value, and some newer ones that I have learned since then, and to infuse my RBA work with different flavors and different additions – I'm thinking of a recipe...you use a basic recipe, and that's your go-to recipe but depending who you're serving, what kind of crowd you're feeding you might add this spice or go to the fridge for that ingredient. Because there are other approaches, frameworks, and tools that can be useful. And I still think being outcome focused is the way to make a difference.

RON: I agree. When I first got into performance measurement, which right around the same time the National Performance Review (the thing that Al Gore led) came out in around 1992, and Osborne and Gaebler came out with "Reinventing Government." There was this new emphasis on outcomes. At the time, government agencies were just counting stuff...outputs...how many transactions they did, how many people they served. There's nothing wrong with counting how many people you serve, but it doesn't tell you much about how effective the program is. Even that much...RBA, for instance, goes a lot further, with its emphasis on population and performance accountability...but even that much...realizing that just counting the number of people you served tells you nothing about the effectiveness of a program...that message came through loud and clear from the national performance review days. Starting to apply that thinking is really important for me. Like you, there is so much that RBA brings to the table, with emphasizing results at the population level and the whole concept of whether anyone is better of (the ultimate outcome)...that stuff still resonates with me. And like you, I like to bring other things to the table when it is appropriate. I don't restrict myself to one framework or one approach. At the same time, you don't want to make a hash of things [laughs] by scrambling things up too much. There's a balance with all of that stuff. I would say that is true whether you're talking about performance stuff or any analytic approach. You have to maintain the inherent logic of the analytic approach you are using, and if you bastardize it too much it becomes less effective.

ANNE: I think that is a good place to stop.

RON: Yep, I'm toast.

ANNE: I know I am...

Appendix 1

		Strongly Disagree				Strongly Agree	Place Selected Number for Each Question in Box, Add to Get Subtoal for Section
	A. Imposter Syndrome	5		4	3	2	1
A1	I sometimes doubt my own abilities.	☐⁵		☐⁴	☐³	☐²	☐¹
A2	People think I know more about data than I really do.	☐⁵		☐⁴	☐³	☐²	☐¹
A3	I feel like a "data fraud."	☐⁵		☐⁴	☐³	☐²	☐¹
A4	I avoid talking about technical details around other data people.	☐⁵		☐⁴	☐³	☐²	☐¹
A5	I avoid situations where I have to work with data with or in front of other people.	☐⁵		☐⁴	☐³	☐²	☐¹
	Subtotal						

		Strongly Disagree				Strongly Agree	Place Selected Number for Each Question in Box, Add to Get Subtoal for Section
	B. Math, Statistics and Developing Data	1		2	3	4	5
B1	I feel comfortable using data collection tools.	☐¹		☐²	☐³	☐⁴	☐⁵

(Continued)

(*Continued*)

		Strongly Disagree				Strongly Agree	Place Selected Number for Each Question in Box, Add to Get Subtoal for Section
	B. Math, Statistics and Developing Data	1	2	3	4	5	
B2	I feel comfortable getting data ready for analysis.	$\bigcirc^1$	$\bigcirc^2$	$\bigcirc^3$	$\bigcirc^4$	$\bigcirc^5$	
B3	I feel comfortable using data analysis software.	$\bigcirc^1$	$\bigcirc^2$	$\bigcirc^3$	$\bigcirc^4$	$\bigcirc^5$	
B4	I feel comfortable working with numbers.	$\bigcirc^1$	$\bigcirc^2$	$\bigcirc^3$	$\bigcirc^4$	$\bigcirc^5$	
B5	I feel comfortable working with complex formulas and statistics.	$\bigcirc^1$	$\bigcirc^2$	$\bigcirc^3$	$\bigcirc^4$	$\bigcirc^5$	
	Subtotal						

		Strongly Disagree				Strongly Agree	Place Selected Number for Each Question in Box, Add to Get Subtoal for Section
	C. Working with Data	1	2	3	4	5	
C1	I feel I have the skills to be an informed data consumer.	$\bigcirc^1$	$\bigcirc^2$	$\bigcirc^3$	$\bigcirc^4$	$\bigcirc^5$	
C2	I feel comfortable interpreting charts and tables.	$\bigcirc^1$	$\bigcirc^2$	$\bigcirc^3$	$\bigcirc^4$	$\bigcirc^5$	
C3	I feel comfortable using data to solve problems.	$\bigcirc^1$	$\bigcirc^2$	$\bigcirc^3$	$\bigcirc^4$	$\bigcirc^5$	
C4	I feel comfortable designing and executing data visualizations.	$\bigcirc^1$	$\bigcirc^2$	$\bigcirc^3$	$\bigcirc^4$	$\bigcirc^5$	

(*Continued*)

(Continued)

		Strongly Disagree				Strongly Agree	Place Selected Number for Each Question in Box, Add to Get Subtoal for Section
C5	I feel comfortable presenting data to others.	$\square^1$		$\square^2$	$\square^3$ $\square^4$	$\square^5$	
Subtotal							

		Strongly Disagree				Strongly Agree	
	D. Sharing/Reporting Data Part 1	5		4	3	2	1
D1	I worry that data about my program or organization, if reported or made public, will be used against us.	$\square^5$		$\square^4$	$\square^3$	$\square^2$	$\square^1$
D2	I worry that data about my program or organization will be unfairly compared with others.	$\square^5$		$\square^4$	$\square^3$	$\square^2$	$\square^1$
D3	I worry that data about my program or organization, if reported or made public, will be embarrassing.	$\square^5$		$\square^4$	$\square^3$	$\square^2$	$\square^1$
D4	I worry that data about my program or organization, if reported or made public, will be misinterpreted.	$\square^5$		$\square^4$	$\square^3$	$\square^2$	$\square^1$
D5	I worry that I may be inadvertently violating some rule, regulation or law when I report or share data.	$\square^5$		$\square^4$	$\square^3$	$\square^2$	$\square^1$
Subtotal							

(Continued)

(Continued)

D. Sharing/Reporting Data Part 2						*Place Selected Number for Each Question in Box, Add to Get Subtoal for Section*

D6	I worry that the data I am able to report is inadequate or does not provide full information about my program or organization.	⃝⁵	⃝⁴	⃝³	⃝²	⃝¹
D7	I worry that the data I am able to share will look visually unsophisticated or outdated.	⃝⁵	⃝⁴	⃝³	⃝²	⃝¹
D8	I worry that I may not report the data correctly and that will lead to misinterpretation of the data.	⃝⁵	⃝⁴	⃝³	⃝²	⃝¹
D9	I worry that my data analysis omits one or two significant variables/ measures that could change my conclusions.	⃝⁵	⃝⁴	⃝³	⃝²	⃝¹
D10	I worry that I will not be able to answer questions about data that is made public.	⃝⁵	⃝⁴	⃝³	⃝²	⃝¹

Subtotal

Overall Score

Appendix 2

	Organizational Self-Assessment	Strongly Agree 1	2	3	4	Strongly Disagree 5
1	My organization uses its identity (e.g., creative, innovative, justice-seeking, people helping) as a reason why we shouldn't focus on data.	○¹	○²	○³	○⁴	○⁵
2	My organization discourages employees from working with data.	○¹	○²	○³	○⁴	○⁵
3	My organization only collects data they are required to collect.	○¹	○²	○³	○⁴	○⁵
4	My organization avoids participating in events where they will be expected to share data.	○¹	○²	○³	○⁴	○⁵
5	My organization discourages making data about the organization or its programs widely available.	○¹	○²	○³	○⁴	○⁵
6	Reports prepared by my organization rarely contain meaningful data.	○¹	○²	○³	○⁴	○⁵
7	My organization has little internal capacity to analyze and report data.	○¹	○²	○³	○⁴	○⁵
8	My organization has few resources devoted to supporting the use of data.	○¹	○²	○³	○⁴	○⁵
9	Leaders in my organization worry that data about our organization will be use against us if it is shared.	○¹	○²	○³	○⁴	○⁵

(Continued)

(*Continued*)

	Organizational Self-Assessment	Strongly Agree 1	2	3	4	Strongly Disagree 5
10	My organization does not have a systematic approach to reviewing data in order to improve programs and services.	○¹	○²	○³	○⁴	○⁵
11	My organization uses concerns about privacy or confidentiality as a reason sharing data "can't be done."	○¹	○²	○³	○⁴	○⁵
12	My organization does not have a public-facing website or portal that allows the public to view important data about the organization or its services.	○¹	○²	○³	○⁴	○⁵
13	My organizations rarely compares or "benchmarks" it performance with the performance of similar organizations, believing that such comparisons might put them in a bad light.	○¹	○²	○³	○⁴	○⁵
14	When employees do take the initiative to collect and analyze data to inform decisions, this behavior is not rewarded or actively encouraged.	○¹	○²	○³	○⁴	○⁵
15	My organization feels more comfortable sharing stories about the success of individual clients than sharing summary data about the performance of programs or services.	○¹	○²	○³	○⁴	○⁵
16	Staff in my organization identify as "non-data" people	○¹	○²	○³	○⁴	○⁵
17	Staff in my organization believe or contend that "data don't matter"	○¹	○²	○³	○⁴	○⁵
18	Staff in my organization tend avoid or defer data tasks	○¹	○²	○³	○⁴	○⁵

(*Continued*)

(*Continued*)

	Organizational Self-Assessment	Strongly Agree 1		2	3	4	Strongly Disagree 5
19	Many staff in my organization openly express their distaste for math and/or statistics.	$\bigcirc^1$		$\bigcirc^2$	$\bigcirc^3$	$\bigcirc^4$	$\bigcirc^5$
20	Staff in my organization rarely use data to make important decisions.	$\bigcirc^1$		$\bigcirc^2$	$\bigcirc^3$	$\bigcirc^4$	$\bigcirc^5$

Overall Score

References

The Nature of Fear

De Becker, G. *The Gift of Fear*. New York: Little, Brown, and Company, 1997.

Harris, R. *The Confidence Gap: A Guide to Overcoming Fear and Self Doubt*. Boulder, CO: Trumpeter Books, 2011.

Nhat Hahn, T. *Fear: Essential Wisdom for Getting through the Storm*. New York: Harper Collins, 2012.

Pressman, T. *Deconstructing Anxiety: The Journey from Fear to Fulfillment*. Lanham, MD: Rowman and Littlefield, 2019.

Cognitive and Group Biases

Cohen, M.D., March, J.G., and Olsen, J.P., 1972. "The garbage can theory of organizational choice," *Administrative Science Quarterly*, vol. 17, no.1, pp. 1–25.

Kahneman, D., Tversky, A., and Slovic, P., *Judgment Under Uncertainty: Heuristics and Biases*. New York: Cambridge University Press, 1982.

Katsikopoulos, K., et al., *Classification in the Wild: The Art and Science of Transparent Decision Making*. Cambridge, MA: MIT Press, 2020.

Continuous Improvement

Brassard, M., and Ritter, D., *The Memory Jogger II*. Methuen, MA: Goal/QPC, 1994.

Wheeler, D., *Understanding Variation: The Key to Managing Chaos*. Knoxville, TN: SPC Press, 1993.

Womack, J.P., and Jones, D.T., *Lean Thinking: Banish Waste and Create Wealth in Your Corporation*. New York: Simon and Schuster, 1996.

Data Display and Visualization

Tufte, E., *The Visual Display of Quantitative Information*. Cheshire, CT: Graphics Press, 1983.

Data Literacy

Bhargava, R., and D'Ignazio, C. Designing tools and activities for data literacy learners. In *Wed Science: Data Literacy Workshop*, Oxford, UK, 2015. https://www.media.mit.edu/publications/designing-tools-and-activities-for-data-literacy-learners/

Fear of Mathematics

Hembree, R. (1990). "The nature, effects, and relief of mathematics anxiety," *Journal for Research in Mathematics Education*, vol. 21, no. 1, pp. 33–46.
Sister Mary Fides Gough, O.P. (1954). "Why failures in mathematics? Mathemaphobia: Causes and treatments," *The Clearing House*, vol. 28, no. 5, pp. 290–294.

Paths to Math Success

Leinward, S., *Principles to Actions: Ensuring Mathematical Success for All*. Reston, VA: The National Council of Teachers for Mathematics, 2014.
Boaler, J., *Mathematical Mindsets: Unleashing Students' Potential through Creative Math, Inspiring Messages and Innovative Teaching*, Hoboken, NJ: Jossey Bass, 2016.

Data Challenges in Performance Measurement

Friedman, M., *Trying Hard Is Not Good Enough*. Sante Fe: Trafford Press, 2006.
Hatry, H., *Performance Measurement: Getting Results*. Washington, DC: Urban Institute, 2006.

McIntyre-Lahner, A., *Stop Spinning Your Wheels: Using Results-Based Accountability to Steer Your Agency to Success.* Clear Impact, 2016.
Schack, R., *Confessions of a Data Scientist...or Warrior Priest: Lessons from 25 Years of Data Science, Performance Measurement, and Decision Support.* Morrisville, NC: Lulu Press, 2019.

Mindfulness

Crane, R. *Mindfulness-Based Cognitive Therapy.* New York: Routledge, 2017.
Kabot-Zinn, J. *Coming to Your Senses: Healing Ourselves and the World Through Mindfulness.* New York: Hyperion Books, 2005.
Kabot-Zinn, J. *Meditation Is Not What You Think: Mindfulness and Why It Is So Important.* New York: Hachette Books, 2018.

Risk Assessment/Analysis

Bourguigon, D. *The Precautionary Principle. Definitions, Applications, and Governance.* European Parliamentary Research Service, 2015.
Gigerenzer, G. *Calculated Risks: How to Know When Numbers Deceive You.* New York: Simon and Schuster, 2002.
Kluger, J. "Why We Worry about the Wrong Things: The Psychology of Risk." *Time*, December 2010.
Lopes, L.A., "Between hope and fear: The psychology of risk." In *Advances in Experimental Psychology*, Vol. 20. Academic Press, 1987. https://doi.org/10.1016/S0065-2601(08)60416-5.

Statistics

Spiegelhalter, D. *The Art of Statistics: How to Learn from Data.* New York: Basic Books, 2019.

Index

Note: **Bold** page numbers refer to tables; *italic* page numbers refer to figures and page numbers followed by "n" denote endnotes.

For Product Safety Concerns and Information please contact our EU
representative GPSR@taylorandfrancis.com
Taylor & Francis Verlag GmbH, Kaufingerstraße 24, 80331 München, Germany